On Whale Island

ALSO BY DANIEL HAYS

My Old Man and the Sea
with David Hays

On Whale Island

Notes from a Place
I Never Meant to Leave

by Daniel Hays

ALGONQUIN BOOKS
OF CHAPEL HILL
2002

Author's Note:

Most of the names and locations in this book have been changed. I even had to change the name of a dog who visited. Any other names resembling those of real people are mostly coincidental. I mean, there are only so many names to go around. —D. H.

Published by
Algonquin Books of Chapel Hill
Post Office Box 2225
Chapel Hill, North Carolina 27515-2225

a division of
Workman Publishing
708 Broadway
New York, New York 10003

Published simultaneously in Canada
  by Thomas Allen & Son Limited.
Design by Anne Winslow.

Grateful acknowledgment is made to the following for permission to reprint copyrighted materials: Aerial photo of Whale Island courtesy of Service Nova Scotia and Municipal Relations, Nova Scotia Geomatics Centre from roll no. 98308, photo no. 263. Drawing of house cross section courtesy of David Hays. © 2002 David Hays.

Library of Congress Cataloging-in-Publication Data
Hays, Daniel, 1960–
    On Whale Island : notes from a place I never meant to leave / Daniel Hays.
      p. cm.
    ISBN 1-56512-345-X
    1. Hays, Daniel, 1960—Homes and haunts—Nova Scotia—Atlantic Coast.   2. Islands—Novia Scotia—Atlantic Coast.
3. Atlantic Coast (N.S.)—Biography.   4. Atlantic Coast (N.S.)—Social life and customs.   5. Country life—Nova Scotia—Atlantic Coast.   6. Simplicity.   7. Hays, Daniel, 1960—Family.   I. Title.
F1039.A74 H39 2002
971.6—dc21   2002018337

10   9   8   7   6   5   4   3   2   1
First Edition

for

WENDY

my joy forever

Contents

On Whale Island

Prologue

Anomie: a state of society in which normative standards
of conduct and belief are weak or lacking; lawless; *also:*
a similar condition in an individual, commonly characterized
by disorientation, anxiety, and isolation

—WEBSTER'S

I GREW UP in New York City and took taxis to
Bloomingdale's, four blocks away. I was always in trouble at school, a condition that these days would be la-
beled with all sorts of letters. At the time, however, I was
just a teacher's bad dream. By sixth grade, the worst year
of my life, I was so anxious about whether I'd be accepted that I would regularly throw up on the way to
school. I carried a dangerous-looking knife, which I
would accidentally drop in front of the girls so they could
see how tough I was. I pretended to be hung over.

When I was fourteen I went to a boarding school in
Vermont, where I did drugs and anything that would
make grown-ups angry. By college I'd already done most
of what a kid could do. I watched classmates discover
drugs and sex and alcohol. I found three good teachers

and took all their classes. I got chased by the campus cops driving my sister's Honda Civic through courtyards—and once into and out the other end of a building.

After I graduated, my dad and I built and then sailed a small boat around South America. The adventure took a year, and we wrote a book about it. At sea I thought about the future and somehow decided to become a doctor. I figured it was a respectable enough career, that I would never have to prove myself once I had the degree. I saw it as a license for not having to question myself. I went back to college to take the science classes I needed, and after one and a half years of struggling, I gave up. I lost more points on one organic chemistry quiz than my lab partner lost during the whole year.

At sea I'd learned that my need to escape from civilization had become as essential as water itself, for I'd realized that I am easily lost. I wanted a wild place where I could hide myself, recharge my vital being and, in so doing, be found. I wanted an island. I wanted a moat of my own, a moat fraught with enough danger to ensure my isolation. With the money my grandmother had given me for medical school, I bought a fifty-acre wilderness island off the coast of Nova Scotia. A car could not come closer than seven miles. The moat was unsheltered Atlantic Ocean.

In the summers I would visit my island. My father and I restored an old shack. I bought an old motorboat, which I kept at a "neighbor's" boathouse for the eleven months of each year that I was away.

Then I went back to school, this time for a master's degree in environmental science. Maybe that would give me enough credentials to quell my self-doubt. During my final internship I drove to Idaho to apprentice as a wilderness guide for troubled teenagers. For the last few hundred miles of the drive, I couldn't help but notice that whenever I pulled off the road to rest, every car that drove past would slow down to see if I was all right. Was I having car trouble? Idaho. I fell in love. People were naturally amiable, and what I had considered normal, having grown up on the East Coast, was actually an unnatural aspect of being human, a muscle that developed under stress.

The job was heaven. I spent weeks dancing through the desert with kids that were too full of life to function in the "real world." We lived under ponchos, drank from streams, and grazed on wild edibles. We ate mice, rats, porcupines, marmots, snakes, crawdads, and anything else we could find. There were natural consequences to being lazy, to feeling victimized, angry, hopeless, or to whatever other flavor of behavioral dysfunction perfected by these teenagers, and those consequences were swift: cold, hunger, and discomfort. Nature did not care about the style of their particular manipulative behavior. When they became aware of the uselessness of proving that they were helpless, stupid, a failure, or innocent of responsibility, growth and change became possible. No longer being successful at controlling the world opens a wonderful door of opportunity.

I was present for hundreds of awakenings. I nudged souls, I got to blow on the coals of simmering fires and be there as they burst into flame, awake with potential and the ability to be themselves. I was a missionary for epiphany, the best job I could ever want.

In Idaho I also met Wendy, blue-eyed and full of life. Being together was simple, effortless, and natural. After the initial lust wore off, we still liked each other. We even became friends. Then we got married.

Wendy came with a son, Stephan. He was nine and had a big laugh like his mom. He was as good a kid as any to become an instant parent to. I'd grown up watching *The Brady Bunch*, and I thought I knew all about parenthood. But there was, as I came to realize, much more that I didn't know. Ugly scenes dealing with the ex for example, a problem I thought happened only to the parents I counseled at work.

The book I wrote with my dad became a best-seller. I got my fifteen minutes of fame, along with a bunch of money. We bought a big house in a resort town. We lived a normal life for two years, and then I got lost somewhere between my twenty-horsepower fuel-injected four-wheel-drive weed whacker and the thirteen separate sprinkler zones surrounding my "estate." I worried a lot about Zone 6. I came to prefer the sprinkler's *fwap fwap fwap* to the rain. I was lost.

I thought of Coleridge: "Will no one hear these stifled groans and wake me?"

• • •

THAT FALL I called my publisher to inquire about my next royalty check. It had been so long since I'd worried about the numbers to the right of the comma that the answer from New York—$5,200—was stunning. That was almost, but not quite, what I needed for just two months of mortgage payments. It seemed my fifteen minutes of fame and riches were over, and I had spent all my riches. I was holding a bottle of Southern Comfort before the phone was hung up.

You probably won't find Southern Comfort in your liquor cabinet, and there is a good reason for this. As a teenager you got just a little too much one time, and the smell or the thought of it triggers something deep in your belly.

The first, second, and third shots burned like a damp cannon fuse in my gut.

I'd been letting a friend keep her horse in our pasture. I hadn't really met Lacy yet; I knew just that she was something called a paint. Feeling quite splashed at the moment, I found this appealing. Her nose was softer than any part of Wendy I'd yet found, so I quickly bonded with her. Although she would not drink from the now half bottle offered, I knew she liked me. In fact, I knew she loved me, and I distinctly remember yelling, "I love you *too*, Wendy" as Lacy walked away with me lying on her back, Wendy upside down. With my head resting on Lacy's fine and musty-smelling rump, I was happy.

There is a little Ahab in us all, not content with any old whale but in search of the big one. Rather than a comfortable walk on an old horse, I *had* to gallop! I'd seen enough TV in my life to know what that looked like, so I sat up and told Lacy that I loved her very much and would she please "giddyap" for me.

I believe what happened next went something like this: horse moves along fence line with fat balding man hugging her mane and murmuring gibberish. Horse moves faster and man bounces up to sitting position, enthusiastically crying "gi' up li'l pony, go a li'l fasser."

It's not so much that I flew over her head and landed like a fillet of seal blubber that upsets me still. It's that Lacy broke my splashy trust in her by stopping on a dime, which was suddenly several feet behind me. *I flew!* I saw my feet silhouetted against clouds, experienced a very abrupt deceleration, and then stared unblinking into a pair of huge horse nostrils. A fly flew out of one.

And that's about when it occurred to me that maybe this lifestyle was no longer working for me. I needed *away,* and that meant distance from the known and the comfortable, distance from habit. It was like the opening of *Moby-Dick:*

Whenever it is a damp, drizzly November in my soul; whenever I find myself involuntarily pausing before coffin warehouses, and bringing up the rear of any funeral I meet; and especially whenever my hypos get such an upper hand of me, that it requires a strong moral principle to prevent me from deliberately stepping into the street, and methodically knocking people's hats off—then, I account it high time to get to sea as soon as I can.

The next day I recited this to Wendy with the passion of a tormented lover. I was prepared to argue, to beg, to fake a breakdown, but before I got there, she said, "So let's go live on Whale Island for a year."

From behind an enormous pile of Legos, Stephan cried, "Cool!"

The house was on the market in a week.

What follows is an account of our life in the only place I know where I could stay forever found. Thoreau wrote, "It is remarkable how long men will believe in the bottomlesness of a pond without taking the trouble to sound it." I find it remarkable how long people will live by and thus accept the values in our civilization without having sounded themselves first.

1. The Journey

> Everything can be found at sea according to
> the spirit of your quest.　　　— CONRAD

JULY 1998

We've been driving for 3,260 miles, two weeks through twelve states. Summer-hot blacktop, the whining of my off-road tires louder than my radio. I like to think that for the whole trip I've been dragging this enormous eraser behind my truck and it has eradicated all of my past, nothing but dust bunnies in my wake. Receding farther and farther in the distance is a twelve-by-thirty-foot storage garage, the tightly packed, stacked, and compressed mass of stuff I've been calling my life for too many years. I secretly pray for a fire.

Wendy and Stephan follow in her new Subaru. I'm driving my beat-up Toyota truck (third engine, mismatched body parts, and 4 percent structural duct tape). I have our two dogs, who pant and drool on me. I find the need for toilets on long drives ridiculous, but breaking a new wife into the enlightened mind-set of squatting is a fearsome task.

"There's a nice tree, honey," I say at a dog break.

"You're taking me to the next gas station, and I want a nice one!" she says. Stephan and I sigh.

WE'VE BEEN CAMPING out every other night, and tonight we stop at a hotel for showers and clean sheets. I've heard that being a parent is like thinking you can catch a landing airplane in a baseball mitt. Perhaps add that it is night and the plane has no landing lights, nor any desire to land. So what do I say to my eleven-year-old boy when he starts masturbating right after the lights go out and he's in a bed just three feet from me and his mother? I pause and pray for just a little divine intervention.

This whole dad thing is new to me. When I got married, I figured that taking on a nine-year-old son would probably be a *little* harder than getting a puppy—after all, I got my dog Bear when he was only twelve days old, so I knew all about bottle-feeding and cleaning up poop. How much harder could a kid be?

So lying there in a hotel room at this obviously pivotal moment in Stephan's life, remembering all I could from Freud, Dr. Spock, Laura Schlessinger, and Kurt Vonnegut, I spoke these words of infinite wisdom: "Hey, *stop that.*"

WE ARRIVE AT the Calais–St. Stephen border, the easternmost crossing into Canada. Having been arrested at this very place five years and thousands of dollars in legal fees ago, I'm a little on edge. As we drive over the bridge, no-man's-land, the dogs sense my unease and begin yelping.

Three years ago I was single and had just (explosively) quit my job. My first book was about to be on the cover of the *New York Times Book Review*. I suddenly had way too much money in the bank. I was "doing a Melville," and as I had been a wilderness-survival instructor for the previous six years, I was packed up to hide on my island until . . . well, I wasn't really sure what I was looking for, or hiding from, but I was clear nobody would be getting in my way. I hadn't counted on a perceptive customs agent. It wasn't that I had that many illegal items with me; it was that the overall picture I painted was—well, an "undesirable" is how one of the many immigration papers described me.

Although *this time* I am not carrying any trip-wire booby traps, smoke flares, or night-vision goggles, I do have what still might appear to be the supplies for a suspect organization. I've packed a set of two-way radios, satellite navigation equipment, 12-volt batteries, a quarter mile of wire, good binoculars, a forty-five-pound box of reconditioned napalm (great for getting wet firewood going), camo clothing, an army first-aid kit (including sutures, pain killers, trauma dressings, and field-surgery tools), two small lasers, and a marine radio with a nine-foot antenna. "You know, just stuff . . ." I hear myself saying defensively to the customs officer.

All goes reasonably well until the officer points and asks me, "What is that for?" Being a teacher at heart I figure a demonstration is in order, so I test my brand-new deluxe imperial fire starter by scraping an impressive shower of sparks in the general direction of this nice uniformed lady. It works better than expected, and although she does not ignite, she does scream.

DAY 1

Another day of driving and we're finally running out of East. The road signs get smaller, the pavement is gone. Turn left before the big ditch, right at the marsh, down the hill almost into the boat shed, left through the really big perpetual puddle, and then the earth ends and all you see is blue-green Atlantic Ocean.

I see Junior standing by the boat shed with his hands on his hips and his usual "Oh jeez, here come the Americans" look. It is as if he'd been waiting for us and standing exactly where I left him sometime last year. Junior is the patriarch of Kingsland, the town on the shore closest to Whale Island. He grew up on Kingsland Island, son of the lighthouse keeper. Then he was the lighthouse keeper for thirty-two years. He and his wife, Becky, raised their three children on the island. In 1979 the lighthouse was automated and they moved to the mainland. The house he lives in now commands a view of the entire harbor.

I have yet to arrive at Junior's dock undetected by land or by sea. If I hit a rock on the way in, beyond his view, he knows. If I take a shortcut over a shallow spot, he knows. He and his family are practically the only folks we know here, and they are plenty.

The kids of theirs whom I know are Mike and Peter. Mike is older, in his forties, and looks like Paul Newman. Peter is shy, the youngest, and difficult to engage in conversation. Both their lives revolve around the water. Lobster, mackerel, sea urchins, scallops, and a lot of hard work provide their income. When I met Peter I immediately felt a kindred spirit in his inability to function around others. On land he is like a fish who can't quite get his gills to work. The third brother—I don't even know his name—is simply not discussed. I don't ask anymore.

IN 1988 A real estate agent showed me a Xerox of an aerial photograph of Whale Island. He handed it to me almost embarrassed, because the property was so far away. "It's damn near impossible to get to," he said. "There's nothing on it but rocks and trees, and it's practically frozen in the ice pack half the year." Perfect, I thought.

Islands are no different than other real estate: there is a complete variety available, with a range of locations and costs. Close to New York City you can spend a million dollars for a half-acre island that connects to the mainland via a small causeway. In 1985 you could have bought John Wayne's old island, near Panama, complete with mansions and an airstrip, for half a million dollars. My father bought an island on the Thames River, in Connecticut, for $25,000 in 1975, less than one acre. Today, several hundred thousand dollars will buy you a twenty-acre island in Maine, but almost all such islands are in sight of the busy coastal roads. Whale Island was the first I could afford, around $80,000 U.S. More important, it was what I'd dreamed of: no lights and no roads, its open shores completely exposed to the ocean. Fifty acres of trees, rocks, and wild. It was a piece of unedited earth, "unimproved," and perfect in every way.

When I was sixteen and in high school, a biology teacher of mine had our class design a garden and wood plot. The assignment was to create an essentially self-sufficient system in which we could live. I remember that fifty forested acres would supply me with seven cords of wood per year forever. That was the wood required to heat a New England farmhouse. I needed to somehow generate electricity; the alternatives were wind, solar, or hydroelectric (best done when a stream or river is nearby, although there are systems that harness tidal energy). I needed a big garden, one hundred feet by fifty feet, if I re-member correctly. Since that time it has always been my desire to live that way. It became a place my mind would wander off to. I wanted to live independently from some-one else's electricity, water, and sewer system. I'd know where my food and my heat came from. I read *Walden Pond*. I wanted "to live deliberately."

That summer my dad and I built a small house on his island in Connecticut. It was a long and hot summer; we worked hard, and by fall the house was habitable. It was gorgeous, rising over the rocks on steel stilts, overlooking the mouth of the Thames River. It blended in with the rocks, and seemed to have always been there. Unfortunately, it was surrounded by a navy shipyard, a chemical factory, and a small but growing city. Long Island protected us from the raw Atlantic. A nuclear-power plant was also nearby, and although all of its lights sort of looked like Paris at night, it was not what I craved.

IN THE SPRING of 1989, when I was twenty-nine, I packed a blow-up boat, an outboard engine, and the only oar I could find into my jeep. I took a ferry from Portland, Maine, to Yarmouth, Nova Scotia, and then drove for half a day to a remote town with the enticing name of Weed Harbor. I hadn't even noticed Kingsland on the map. A spring gale was just getting started, and I'd never seen it snow parallel to the ocean before. Actually, it was worse than parallel: it seemed to snow up from the ocean.

I asked several guys around the dock if they would take me out to Whale Island. The response was immediate.

"No, not in this wind, no way."

I waited.

"Try one of them Carters in Kingsland—they'll go out in anything," one man finally volunteered.

I have since found that anyone in Kingsland who must mention Weed Harbor at all will include some colorful and descriptive metaphors in their response. Who knows how far back in time this feud goes? Nova Scotia was visited long before Columbus by Vikings, and Weed Harbor is only a day's row from the suspected first settlement.

Maybe Weed Harbor boys are direct descendants of the Vikings and their barbaric ways. It would explain a lot, according to the Kingsland boys, anyway.

I drove farther east for another hour and found Kingsland. The town seemed deserted, literally at the end of a road. There were no stores, no phone booths, no traffic. But I did see beautiful workboats in the small harbor. I found a truck whose hood was warm, and in the building that was closest to it I first met Peter. He was building lobster pots, and my first thought was that he'd been doing it all winter, standing in his shed surrounded by rope, wood, wire, and tools. I introduced myself and asked would he take me out to Whale Island? He mumbled something about his boat being "laid up for a while," and pointed me toward a house, where I eventually found his brother Mike. Again, I introduced myself and asked if he'd take me out.

"By Jesus, what the hell would you want to go out in this snot for?"

"Fifty dollars?" I suggested. He looked at me quizzically.

"And a bottle of rum," I hastily added.

Mike took me out through the storm. He didn't even flinch. He had to test the rum, to make sure I wasn't pulling something on him, and then I had to be polite. Along the way, I saw the ocean as one finds it only at sea: waves as big as school buses surging over barn-sized rocks. Great masses of ocean, so unquestionably powerful that I always feel humble in their presence. People often talk of man *against* the sea, which to my mind is as counterintuitive as challenging gravity. A storm is a magnificent glimpse into the heart of nature to be regarded with wonder, not ego.

And that storm has made all the difference.

I BOUGHT WHALE ISLAND later that week. My passion and enthusiasm, combined with a complete lack of business sense, were not assets during the purchase negotiations. I was played like a fiddle. I closed the deal paying somehow twice the initial asking price. I justified that allowing myself to be manipulated by a savvy European businessman was evidence that I was incapable of associating with the real world. I actually *needed* an island, I reasoned, for my own safety.

That summer my father and I pitched a tent for two weeks on Whale Island. We explored the island, both by land and by sea. We spent hours lost in the thick fog on the small boat Junior lent us. We found ruins of previous buildings. We rebuilt a small fishing shed, the only structure still standing. Various lobstermen would stop by to yarn with us. The shed was in the island's only harbor, and the lobstermen had some of their traps just twenty feet from our tent. Slowly, and with caution, they spoke with us, and the history of the island was revealed.

Almost everyone had a story involving a relation who had once owned Whale Island. "My great-granddaddy bought it for two dollars in 1910, and he always said he paid too damn much. He fished here in the summers," one man told us. "I remember a shipwreck when I was little, a boatload of molasses, thick as oil it was. Her anchor's still on the shore over there," he said, pointing. Another spoke of coming here for picnics as he grew up, finding parts of shipwrecks on the beach, and how "a crazy American once lived here, I think he was the last fellow to winter on the island, didn't get on too good with anybody. Them windows you're replacing there was *shot* out, you know."

The stories kept pouring in. "Three men was buried on the north shore. I remember a cross used to mark the spot. I came here with my daddy when I was little. He'd leave me ashore while he pulled traps in the narrows there. Of course that stretch of island was washed away in '56." Another told us of a herd of deer who swam out and lived on the island for a while. In 1928 there was a fire. These stories left me wondering how my own time on the island would be described to future generations.

My father is a terrific designer. He actually learned the trade by designing stage sets on Broadway in 1955. The eight-by-eleven-foot shed we rebuilt became as snug as the two sailboats we'd built years before. We planked the inside with pine, made bunks and a kitchen, and installed lots of hooks so wet clothing could dry. We put in a tiny woodstove. We put in windows and a new roof. A few years later it fed eight friends for the five summer weeks it took us to build the main house.

There is no easy way to summarize the building of our home: 100 pounds of nails; 150 pounds of nuts, bolts, and washers; between 12 and 15 tons of lumber; 1 ton of cement; and 100 gallons of water for the cement. In all, the house cost me under $20,000 to build. The friends who came to help stayed about a week each. We worked—my father, the friends, and I—from sunup till sundown. We made about eighty trips to the shore to pick up our supplies, a total of over eleven hundred miles, or nearly the distance between New York and Miami.

We unloaded much of the lumber onto a rocky peninsula closer to the house than our main harbor. We could do this only at high tide, and the sea had to be calm. Probably a third of everything fell into the water at least once. One bag of cement is still visible at low tide. There are 652 steps up a steep and winding path leading to the house. Friends named this "the Trail of Tears" after a week of carrying almost half of the future house on their backs. This was a long, hot summer.

Now, bringing my new family to this place for the first time, I remember how the main house is still not quite finished. The fishing shed will act as a guest house, and maybe a retreat for later on, when cabin fever strikes.

No road—or even footpath—can follow the coast between the harbors of Kingsland and Weed Harbor. The mainland is rife with bogs and inlets, some cutting way inland. These natural walls keep the roads far away. Whale Island is on the outer curvy part of a bulge of wilderness land along the eastern shore. From the island we see no sign of civilization except, at twelve-second intervals, the flash of the Kingsland lighthouse. By boat it is seven miles to the closest road, in Kingsland. There is no way to walk along the coast toward the island from either town without having to ford the inlets, and you would probably die from mosquito bites.

Most of Whale Island is forever hidden. The trees are so dense that penetrating the thicker parts is possible only by walking backward. You just lean and push like hell, and the trees snap back into place behind you. If not for the constant sound of the ocean you would become lost after about ten feet, at which time where you came from would no longer be visible, gone in solid walls of dark green. Once, determined to get to the center of the island, I bravely launched myself into the void. After only about two minutes I walked right off a cliff. It took me a full twenty seconds to "fall" the ten or fifteen feet through the clutching spruce trees. I landed, if it can be called that, safe and happy on thick moss. I climbed up the way I had come and headed for the shore's constant music. I have not tried again.

From space Whale Island looks like an aggravated baby pterodactyl. When I look at a map of it, I always wait for a twitch, or I listen for a screech reminiscent of the cartoon *Jonny Quest*. The island is quite alive for me.

I am still fascinated by how each stretch of the coast is different. It's as if shores from around the world have been collected and reassembled here to highlight the verities of nature. Some areas are huge sheets of bare granite with thick veins of quartz running through. A few hundred feet farther along there is nothing but baseball-sized rocks, smoothed over time. My favorite is a stretch of basketball-sized rocks, which are smoothed and rearranged only during the biggest storms. (As they constantly shift, you have to hop with agility on these rocks, pretending each half fall is just the beginning of the next hop.) There is also a small sandy beach, a flat rock beach composed only of skipping stones, a marsh, a beach of pebbles, some areas where dirt falls directly into the sea, and some jagged steep-sided inlets where I can barely hang on. And there is one beach where all the ocean seems to deposit its flotsam, a terrific place to find buoys and pieces of wood for building stuff. There are unbroken rock peninsulas of solid bedrock, earth bones. There are pools where rainwater collects, tidal pools full of squirming life, and flat stretches of rock where the seagulls come to drop and crack open sea urchins or crabs so they can get to the soft meat inside.

NOW AT JUNIOR'S DOCK, the end of the road, our two dogs explode from the truck in a flurry of pee urgency. They run directly for Junior. Abby is an overbred neurotic Airedale. Bear is a studly Idaho sheepherding mutt. They are in love with each other. Both engulf Junior, completely disregarding his cool Irish demeanor. Abby leaps toward his face like a dart, her tongue desperate for a proper introduction.

The air is clean and I fill my lungs deeply, starting at that exact moment a new life. We are at the end of the road, with everywhere to go before us.

"Yup. Here we are. You better like us 'cause you're

stuck with us for a year," I say. Junior almost smiles. "Well, by Jeezus, I'm willing to *put up* with you is all." (High praise, I think.)

Junior's boathouse is the hub of Kingsland. I love to stand in it with my eyes closed, smelling a hundred years of sea life. Shelves overflow with the sort of gear you see being used in the old *Captain Courageous* movie with Spencer Tracy: anchors, buckets of tar, buoys, nets, pulleys, crab traps, sails, spars, pails of hardware. The place does more than smell; it tastes, rich sea broth from a long time ago.

With Junior's help we uncover our aluminum motorboat from the dark depths of his shed. I always leave it there between my visits, and since it's a well-used boathouse, many things are placed, temporarily at least, on the boat. "Uncovering" the boat is more like "finding" the boat under fishnets, boxes, and great coils of rope. There is a ramp leading directly from the shed's back barn doors into the sea. The boat is light enough for the four of us to nudge her along. Once she is on the ramp she slides eagerly into the shallows.

The outboard engine is a 25-horsepower with no fancy attachments. A three-foot section of PVC pipe is duct-taped to extend the steering arm so I can stand up to see over the bough while steering. The boat is a seventeen-foot workboat that I bought from Junior, old and scratched up just right. I haven't felt her in the water for a full year, and I remember that when I float on any ocean I am floating on the whole world's surface. I become calm, content just to be. This is only Stephan's second time seeing the Atlantic, and he's off playing with a starfish. Wendy seems a little afraid, and I hug her tightly.

We overload the boat with too much of our stuff and are off. Three humans, two dogs, and the first load of four hundred pounds of "the bare necessities" of life. The boat is weighed down, our outboard not powerful enough to allow us to plane over the water. We surge ahead like a brick, but a happy brick. A small wave slaps the boat and splashes us. Finally.

Our driveway travels along unspoiled coast. If our boat were light, it would take us about twenty minutes. Today it is closer to an hour, and we all watch as the shore's shifting mysteries slowly unfold. Since last summer there has obviously been some stormy weather. New trees are washed up well beyond the high-tide mark. House-sized boulders have been moved.

From a mile away, as we round Strawberry Point, Whale Island appears. Often shrouded in fog, it is low and surrounded by a ring of gray-and-white granite shoreline. There are several outlying ledges to avoid. Sometimes during big storms one of these, usually a good ten feet below the surface, will be exposed between massive surges of ocean. The thundering waves breaking on this ledge turn an area the size of a football field into a chaos that one cannot help but think of as unleashed fury. Today there is no sign of this, and we motor right over the submerged Goliath. The cold water is especially clear this early in the summer: rocks and fish quite sharply defined to about ten feet, shapes for another fifteen feet. In many places the winter's ice has scratched all marine growth from the bottom, and the rocks are mostly white, clean granite.

We round the rocks protecting the harbor. In the shallows we see the fish, crabs, and rocks that will become familiar with our family as the year goes on. Our harbor is an underwater world teeming with life and activity. I cut the engine and we glide onto the beach. There is nothing like the feeling of a small boat as it skids onto a gravel shore; you have arrived with certainty.

Stephan has not grown up on boats as I have, so he must learn all of the basic rules of seamanship from me. I ask him to jump to the shore and hold the bow. But he is not in the front of the boat when I ask him, so he jumps off the stern. He lands in the water up to his waist. I cringe, and Wendy says, "Stephan, you're all wet now, you'll catch cold!" He couldn't care less. He's ecstatic. Wendy is fixated on how she'll have to wash his salty clothes and how he might get sick. I am wondering where I failed. How could any kid that I live with jump into the water like that? I am preparing a lecture on how to stay dry when Stephan screeches, "*Yahoo-eee!*" and runs up the beach to chase a seagull, forgetting about the boat and everything else in the world.

"He's just a little guy," Wendy says, noticing my reaction to the nautical blasphemy that has just occurred. It is not appropriate to leap out of a boat that needs assistance to chase seagulls. It is just *not done.*

"Hey, bonehead!" I yell. "Get your little ass back here and hold the boat!"

Grinning, and with water sloshing out of his boots, Stephan runs back just as a small wave turns the boat sideways and carries her up to the beach.

We unload a huge pile of stuff as the dogs tear up the smooth beach with as much enthusiasm as can be contained in their two bodies. The new smells must be wonderful to them, especially after having been stuck so long in my truck. Their wet noses flash in the sunlight.

The first order of business for me is making the boat safe. Under a tree, right where I left it after last summer's visit, is a coil of rope. I tie one end to an eyebolt that I secured to a van-sized boulder in '93 (I had to rent a generator and a big hammer drill to do that). I launch the boat (mumbling childishly under my breath at Stephan) and let her drift across the small harbor to another eyebolt similarly embedded on the other shore, and tie up to that one too. Between the two eyebolts is 300 feet of rope led through a pulley at each end. By securing the boat to any place along that continuous line, about 150 feet between shores, I can haul the boat out to the middle of the harbor and then knot the rope to the eyebolt. This way she's in the middle of the small bay, where the water is deepest. I can leave her there safely during all but the worst weather.

We carry food, clothes, tools, books, and even Legos over a quarter mile of treacherous roots. I cut this trail years ago from the harbor on the east of the island to the south-facing shore, and it's a bit curvy, *meandering* almost. (Junior's comment was "What were you, drunk?") We all pull some muscles.

The hinges to the door are rusted almost solid, but we eagerly open the house and breathe in last year's air. We stand together, just inside the door. The atmosphere is thick and wonderful.

Wendy and I put our bags down and look at each other. "Wendy, we are home!" I pronounce. Her smile, with the ocean, the dancing sunlight—it's a perfect moment. She hugs me tightly. Then Stephan (with the intuition of an only child who might not for a moment be the absolute center of attention) tries to join us. He gets about halfway up the stairs before slipping with his box of Legos into a colorful heap at the bottom. Wendy and I peer down the stairs. After a pause, Stephan holds up a green animally looking Lego and cries out, "I found my Lego alligator, I found him!"

Small organized anthills litter the floor. At first we step around them, as if honoring all their hard work. Upstairs, I examine a pile and see that it is light blue, obviously insulation that has rained down from the roof. I guess the ants have been tunneling up there all year. I wonder just how much insulation is left? Guess we'll find out come winter.

Before nuzzling down into our blankets on the hard floor, I encourage Wendy and Stephan to keep a journal of this year. "For you, it's required," I tell Stephan. "Being able to recognize your feelings, thoughts, the best or worst part of the day, whatever you want. Just mean it. It's important to express yourself. One day you will be glad you did this, and if not, you can burn it all then."

I turn to Wendy. "And please don't just write when you are pissed off at me. I know that's when you usually write, but when you are old and rereading it—I mean, I do good stuff too, right?"

She looks at me with raised eyebrows. "If you want a positive leading role in my journal, you can start right now and be quiet."

Later, I sigh all the way down to my toes, melting into the moment that I've been dreaming of for two years. I follow the huggable moon's reflection to its origin, seemingly just out of reach. (Thank God for that, or I'm sure we'd find a way to ruin even the moon . . .)

Stephan

I had to carry boxes, sacks, books, food, pillows, and a mattress.

Enough about the bad stuff—let's talk about the good stuff. The moon is beautiful tonight; when it came up its light on the water made it look like there was a yellow road from here to the moon.

Wendy

We are on Whale Island!

I am a little nervous about being here, so far out of my element. I am going to miss baths terribly. There is a beautiful full moon tonight reflecting off the water—it's just incredible. I am exhausted. There's going to be a lot of hard work this year.

2. Moving In

> I would rather sit on a pumpkin and have it all to
> myself than be crowded on a velvet cushion.
>
> —THOREAU

DAY 2

Our house rests on a hill roughly forty feet above high
tide. It is the highest point on the island and two hundred
feet inland. The first floor is almost completely wrapped
in dense trees, and it is cozily dark. The second floor is
level with the treetops. Sitting on the roof puts you at
about sixty-five feet above sea level. Facing south and east
we look out over the Atlantic, nothing but ocean between
us and Africa. Facing north we overlook our island, and
then the mainland wilderness, only a few football fields
from one of the island's peninsulas. It is a magnificent
green of rolling hills and rocky outcrops. Dropped by receding glaciers, huge boulders are strewn about the low
hills.

By its very nature this rugged, windswept, wild, and
even dangerous landscape demands the same attention
and awe as the sea. It must be respected and even loved.

To want to "challenge" and "conquer" this landscape is missing the beauty and heart of it. Stupid too.

Our home is made of tongue-and-groove pine plank-ing, cedar shingles, and lots of glass. The footprint of the ground floor is fourteen by sixteen feet, with the top floor about half a foot more cozy on all sides because the walls lean in. The house resembles a Dutch windmill without the vanes. If not for the thick trees, Don Quixote would love it. (Junior says, "By Jeezus, the farther away you get, the better it looks.") The upstairs is mostly windows, and the only section of wall that is not thick glass has an old porthole in it, bought at a salvage yard. (I often wonder what sights and impressions have passed through its por-tal.) At our elevation above the ocean of around fifty-five feet, on a clear day the horizon is nine miles away. Using a calculator and that funny pi button, I figure that we overlook one hundred and thirty square miles of waves and uninterrupted magnificence.

The inside of the house is still pretty bare. On the ground floor there is a bunk bed my father started to build before we left last summer. This will be for Stephan. As soon as he can tack up a blanket so as to make it into a dark cave he'll be happy. There is a small bathroom next to the woodstove, its door stained glass that brings a sense of colorful magic into the room. Otherwise the downstairs is empty, and although there are three win-dows and a porthole like the one upstairs, the room is pretty dark. You can hear the trees rubbing on the walls when the wind blows.

A steep-enough-to-hurt-you-if-you-slip staircase leads up to what will become the living room, kitchen, bedroom, dining room, library, playroom, and sunroom, all in a space barely big enough to park two old-style VW Bugs. This is how the best sailboats are put together, and my father has an uncanny way of designing small heavens. I have some ideas and sketches we drew up last year. A sperm-whale rib recovered from our shore is our banister. Last year my father and I brought out a handsome wood-burning cookstove, which has been converted to propane. Another whale bone, the inside of the jaw, is our sink. Two director's chairs face each other. There's nothing else but the ant piles.

THE WORD OF THE DAY is *bin*. We have twelve hundred pounds of "only essential" gear boxed in blue, green, and purple Tupperware-esque bins. A month ago we had a tweny-one-hundred-square-foot home. We downsized to a thirty-by-twelve storage unit. Then a truck and a car. Now it's thirty-two rubber boxes. We make two trips back to Junior's dock. He *always* meets us. Sometimes he helps with all the carrying, and sometimes he just gives advice: "You can park the Subaru in my driveway, but hide that ugly truck in them bushes, there past the dock."

I've already unpacked my books. They line the floor under the east and south windows. I expect I will have to move them a dozen times before their shelves are built. And that is something I love, to handle books.

When I think of what living here will be like, I think of the stories in these already damp books. What do I need from our culture that I do not already have the best of before me? Farley Mowat, Kazuo Ishiguro, Brontë, Mark Twain, Vonnegut, David Duncan, Dumas, Jane Goodall, Ayn Rand, Rudyard Kipling, John Irving, Voltaire, Annie Proulx, James Clavell, D. H. Lawrence, Douglas Adams, Tom Robbins, Gabriel García Márquez, Defoe, and Kierkegaard. These are my roommates, these are the friends I will drink coffee with. I have little use for the McWorld. I have a seven-mile driveway, which I pray will shield me. Leave me with my friends!

DAY 3

Waking up on Whale Island is like being led by a tipsy angel from one world to another. I finish all my dreams here. The angel playfully tugs on my soul, using the glow from the sunrise, a seagull's squawk, or maybe the rumble from a big wave—she gently lays me back into my body. I always have the time to take two or three deep breaths before opening my eyes, testing the equipment, stretching.

When I sit up I am greeted by the world. Level with the treetops I look down on sparrows swooping in and out of the branches. The tide, the new rising moon, the clouds, the wind—these greet me. These are my allies. The whole planet is laid out before me and available for whatever adventure the day will take me on.

By comparison, living in society seems to require an

alarm clock. Primarily assembled from angst and fish anuses, these contraptions, regardless of your soul's whereabouts, will slap and assault you into a pitiful state of what passes for consciousness. Your first sight is the Time, an arrangement of molecules on the clock's face to whom you will be enslaved for the rest of the day. You may as well call him "master." Next, a pile of dirty clothes on the floor, a knocked-over glass of water, and so forth, until you are so overwhelmed with despair that to prevent hurling yourself through the window, you must ignore your personal bill of rights, put on an acceptable frown, and go about your business, disregarding the pleas from your increasingly timid soul.

TODAY IT RAINED from the east like it really wanted us to get wet. The house leaked in fifty-seven places, fifty-four of them over Stephan's bunk. Wendy and I don't have a bed yet. We're just sleeping on the floor. I'm not sure where to put a bed without taking up most of our living room.

Wendy and Stephan heroically transported the last of our supplies from the harbor, trekking the narrow path to the house another ten times each. I built shelves, and Wendy tried to organize the growing plethora of boxes and bags.

After some peanut-butter sandwiches we all walk around the island and are wide-eyed at the beauty, even forgetting to name everything we see. As humans we tend to conceptualize rather than experience, and forgetting to put labels on things is a good indication that we are truly alive.

Despite whatever hardships Stephan has suffered with-out much of a father, he has clearly survived, pure kid. Living for right now, he runs from the rocks to the water to the trees to the moss, from anywhere to everywhere. He is so happy that he could be the third dog.

"Look at this! Wow, *hey look!*" he says, triumphantly squeezing something until goo spurts out.

"Can we eat this?" he begs.

For a wonderful moment I transcend myself and view the five of us from above. The dogs running in circles around the humans, the two bigger humans loving the lit-tler one. They are joined together in a moment of bliss, of calm ecstasy.

I am rudely slapped back into my body as a fingerload of the previously mentioned goo is thrust under my nose.

"Does it smell okay? Can we eat it for dinner? What is it? Are there any more?"

I think to myself that if it stays this easy, I can do it, be a dad. Even if it gets harder, all I will have to do is just re-member this moment. He's a child, he's new to the world. Love him.

Back at the house I finish putting in our toilet, a sur-prisingly important component of "luxury." Hanging off the back of the house, it sits in a separate room with the stained-glass door. It's a boat toilet: the waste gurgles down a three-foot straight pipe into a thirty-five-gallon drum buried in the soil. I shot holes in the drum before burying it, so that it drains into the earth. It's a great thing to know exactly where our wastes go; on an island there is no real concept of "away" or "that's somebody else's problem."

Electricity, cable TV, city water, and a telephone are nonexistent in this, my kingdom. In fact, avoiding TV and what I call unconscious consumption are the most desirable qualities of being here. I don't want the finer aspects of our culture's pathology funneled into Stephan's brain through a television. TV is a clump of perverted perceptions, and most of us arrange our living rooms around it, and worship it. And phones!! I do not want to ever, ever be interrupted by a phone's ringing when I am on this island in the presence of nature.

By evening the sky clears for a wonderful sunset and full moonrise. Stephan and I prepare a broccoli-and-cheese soup for dinner, the first real cooking we've done in our new kitchen. I open the can, and then Stephan knocks it over. Stephan turns on the gas, and I singe an eyebrow in the ensuing explosion. We are a good team.

The stove seems so elegant and out of place. I polish the white porcelain knobs as the soup boils over. Stephan asks how long we should let it do that, and I say, "This is our island. We can boil stuff as long as we want to. As long as your mother is downstairs, anyway."

"Is that why we're here, so we can make the rules?"

"Yes," I say contentedly.

The moon climbs higher into the night.

Stephan

We really cleaned up the house today. It looks much better. I got a really bad scrape. I love the island, I love it!

3. Building Our Nest

The secret of realizing the greatest fruitfulness and
greatest enjoyment of existence is: to live dangerously!
Build your cities on the slopes of Vesuvius! Send your
ships out into uncharted seas! Live in conflict with
your equals and with yourselves!

— NIETZSCHE

DAY 4

My creative self is fully awake, wonderfully alive in my
body. While working on a kitchen shelf, I run down to
"Wash-up Point" to find a weather-beaten piece of driftwood. I intuitively know that it will fit, and feel not so
much a successful hunter as I do a willing recipient. Back
in the house the wood settles into its new home perfectly,
as if it had been waiting for me on the beach, which leads
me to wonder about the storm that brought it here.

Sometimes I like to have a drink at night to help settle
my soul back into my body. I love to wander about the
rocks. Sometimes I fall, missing a step like I was already
onto the next, and I land so content that I am cushioned
by the rocks, gently brought down and embraced, I feel,

by love rather than gravity. I walk a bit more, and then I lie on a mat of moss, where I settle so deeply into its sponginess that when I leave I feel like I'm waking from a lover's embrace. I want to lie motionless until I am dug up a Bog Man.

DAY 6

As I work on the house I discover one of life's everlasting truths: invention is caused not necessarily by necessity; laziness and stupidity are equally, if not more, important. For example, the construction of a small spice shelf begins with the realization, as I'm sitting on the floor, that the stinging sensation in my thigh is caused by an oddly shaped piece of shingle with a screw in it left over from a small shelf for a candle that I have just completed. I pull the screw out of my leg, angrily looking around for whom or what to blame. I hold the piece firmly—perhaps so that it cannot escape—and I see an area of open wall under a window easily within reach. Because all the beams in the house taper toward the roof, there are always weird angles to wedge bizarre shelves into. I squeeze the shingle enthusiastically into place, and it cracks. Now comes the really stupid part: having forgotten *why* I am putting an unneeded shelf nowhere useful, I roll over (laziness now dictating that under no circumstances will I actually *stand up*) and grab another shingle, which is too big. Quickly, perhaps to prevent accidental thought, I split the shingle by smashing it against my forehead. Now it's a perfect fit! And so, with a little blood dribbling down my face, the job is finished.

DAY 8

The bed Wendy and I build is a simple four-by-six-foot piece of plywood supported by a frame of two-by-four-inch planks; i.e., it's a platform with a futon on it. During the day we hoist it up into the ceiling rafters by two ropes and a creative tangle of pulleys. "Raising the bed" takes two of us and has to be done with some coordination, often lacking before coffee. We then tie the two ropes off on cleats mounted on the wall. Thus every day starts with a little nautical activity, making fast and coiling down, which makes me smile inside. When we lower the bed at night, it rests on two sawhorses (which we put on the bed before we hoist it up in the morning). Our nest settles perfectly at about waist height. Lying down, we are level with the treetops. Moon, sun, stars, planets, birds, clouds, and ocean are the art hung on our walls.

DAY 11

Today is roof-repair day, and I spill tar all over. Some of it lands where shingles have been blown off, and that's why I can consider myself doing "repairs," because I spill *strategically*. Wendy throws requested tools up to me, and I balance precariously on the edges. I install rain gutters to catch our water, funneling it into hoses, which lead down to the two fifty-five-gallon drums that I bought at the old fish plant in town. They rest under the stairs, and I put a leftover piece of plywood over them to make a workbench.

Quote of the day, immediately following Stephan's carrying some of the groceries from the boat to the house.

I say: "Stephan, why are all the eggs broken?" He replies, "Because *Mom* never told me where all the roots were, and I tripped over four of them."

The thing is, when he makes these excuses, he completely believes them! Is this a typical twelve-year-old? What's going on in his head? Where is the instruction book?

Stephan

We went into town again today. We left the dogs on the island and I was worried about them. We had fun. Lots of carrying.

DAY 12

Abby the "dog" bursts into the house having rolled in last summer's outhouse pit. Then, standing in the middle of the room as we watch in fear, she vomits eleven crabs. We know it's eleven because Stephan proudly recounts having fed them to her. I can't remember if crabs are arthropods or anthropoids, but hell, there were *lots* of legs (divisible by six, eight, or ten).

The best thing I can say about Abby right now is that it sure is cool, when it is dark out, to shine a flashlight in her ear and see her eyes light up from the inside as if she is possessed. Given her level of intelligence, I sometimes tell Wendy, any possession would be welcome. I call Abby the "dog" because an Airedale is about as smart as a bag of hammers. Those who disagree with me are a special group of people—Airedale owners—and they will use words like "independent," "stubborn," and even "slightly dyslexic" to explain why their dog responds to only about a third of their suggestions.

Bear is different; he is thoughtful and will watch a sunset. He is a mix of Australian shepherd, border collie, and some blue. He is unfixed and quite alpha, full of primitive wolflike traits that Airedale owners would be shocked to witness. Like shitting on bushes—a scent mark—and kicking up dirt after he pees—an exclamation point. He can raise his hackles really impressively, making himself seem hugely overmuscled. He even pees on top of my pee and will run a quarter mile to do so when he sees me in the early morning peeing off the second-floor porch into the treetops.

I've caught Bear being foolish only a couple of times since he's grown up. Once he was enjoying a scratching from me so thoroughly that he let himself blissfully roll off the bed. He landed in an embarrassed heap and pretended he had done so on purpose by not moving and gently sighing, as if this was simply his *new* preferred resting spot. Then yesterday I gave him a piece of rawhide to munch on and he was so excited that when he hunkered down to eat it he left his hind legs standing, a right triangle with a wagging tail.

DAY 13

Beautiful sunrise and rotten morning of the evil stepfather versus Stephan. Things have not been as rosy as I may have been pretending.

I stumble downstairs, before coffee, before going to the bathroom, and I trip over a pile of soaking clothes. I crash into the inarguable iron of the woodstove, my shin becoming alive with white pain. The cables that carry this message to my brain overheat, and Stephan is awakened from his sleep by my screaming something like "GOD-DAMNIT! What the hell, STEPHAN! Get up and go hang your wet clothes up, I can't believe this! I asked you twice last night to hang this up outside, was that too much for you? Is it un-goddamn-reasonable of me to ask you this? Does your mother have to do everything for you? Hello, does anything I say matter?"

He screams, *"Why don't you just go away, leave me alone, I hate you!"*

I have a strong urge to explode, just blow up into small and harmless pieces, my consciousness fully dispersed.

"Living with you is like sharing a cage with a big monkey!" I yell back.

"Then go away. Leave me alone."

Silence.

Stephan's face is honest with his emotions, tears spill from his eyes, and a sob escapes. My face, I know, is contorted into some nightmare's devil. Stephan runs out of the house and slams the door. A pane of glass falls to the floor and breaks.

It is a shame the technology does not yet exist for either Stephan or me to be frozen solid and not thawed until the other has matured a little.

I ask Wendy: "I can tell there is something I'm supposed to be doing, something I can't *feel*, but I can't grasp enough of it to know. What is it?"

"It's love. He's just a little guy, and you treat him like he's gotta meet your own standards to be loved, like he has to earn it from you and can't even keep any extra in the bank for a grumpy moment."

Ouch, that's true.

Here I am trying to be in a friendship with this alien, and I'm worrying more about protecting my feelings than about his. I've been treating him like I would a rock, and not surprisingly, with my emotions so contorted, I haven't been able to write, make love to Wendy, or communicate in any way that feels right. I take sleeping pills so I don't lie awake hating myself for failing, for not being as good a dad as my dad was.

Still, I am utterly unable to say, "I'm sorry, I was wrong."

Wendy

I haven't written for a long time. Sometimes I find myself getting depressed out here. Stephan is getting on my nerves, even though he is only being an eleven-year-old human.

Yesterday I got so angry at Daniel that I wasted about a gallon of water on doing the dishes, and boy was he pissed.

I think I will probably survive; it is just very difficult. I hate having to clean up sawdust every day, and it gets into the food. Daniel says it's good for our digestion.

We have been walking around the island almost every day. It is a great time for us to be a family.

Stephan

Me and Mom just got back from walking around the island. I tightened all of the bolts today so that the house would not fall apart.

DAY 14

Last night Stephan tightened all of the 386 bolts that keep our house in temporary entropy denial (every year the wood dries a little more, so they need attention). He then knocked over about a gallon of leftover borscht, which rained down the steps and onto a clothes pile, all the tools, and both dogs. When the red wave ceased there were two perfect dry dog outlines on the floor, and two reddish shapes could be seen running into the forest biting each other, trying to eat small pieces of sausage off of one another.

I just breathed deeply and went outside.

Today is *windmill* day. Nova Scotia has no shortage of wind. I bought an $800 marine windmill from a company in Arizona. It's as heavy as a medium watermelon and has a four-foot propeller span. It is white and streamlined, wires lead away from it, and when it spins it produces electricity, a luxury item we use now mostly for listening to music.

We mount the windmill on the roof and run wires into two 12-volt car batteries. With a hideous confusion of auto cigarette-lighter plugs and extension cords, these will power our radio and CD player, a VHF radio, a battery charger for all the flashlights' double-A's, and even an old Apple laptop. We also have three small portable solar panels. These are each three by two feet and flexible (like thick leather) and can be plugged into the system when it is sunny and windless. One panel in bright sunlight will play the radio on medium volume but not quite spin a CD. The big batteries, once full, will run everything for a couple of weeks without any charging. Our needs are minimal. Our lighting is from kerosene lamps and candles, a warm and friendly light.

DAY 15

Since our house is the highest thing around I figured the roof was the best location for the windmill, as that's obviously where the wind is. Big mistake. Last night the wind blew hard from the east—maybe thirty knots—and it was like sleeping in a subway station. The house shook and vibrated and seemed to scream during the gusts. Not a timid scream—a full-throated "There's a monster standing next to my bed" type of scream. This morning there were waves in my coffee. I guess it's time for plan B.

In the afternoon I get the whale-jawbone sink working, and I cannot help but ponder the fate of this leviathan. In the spring thaw of 1992 two dead sperm whales washed up on the island. We are close to the southern limit of the ice pack, where the ocean surface can freeze in solid sheets several miles wide. Apparently whales sometimes get caught underneath and drown. That spring Junior made one of his rare phone calls to me in Idaho with the warning "Yep, you got some dead whales washed up on the island there."

Two sperm whales are equal to about 120 feet and over a hundred tons of dead meat. Talk about a lawn problem. Believe it or not, one can get acclimated to having two tractor trailers of rotting meat just outside the front door. It took two years for all of it to erode. *And then the bones appeared!* We're talking major bones here, like a skull that seats twelve, a vertebra that makes a killer toilet seat, a rib seven feet long for a stair railing, disks made into plates, and even an assortment of Calderesque art, seven-foot rib mobiles hanging from the trees. The inside of the jawbone is shaped like an oval, and it makes a great sink. I attach one end to a pulley, so that to drain it we just hoist it a few inches. The water goes down a funnel (where the teeth were) with a melodious gurgle. It runs into the trees, and when food clogs it up it is always fun to try to fool Wendy or Stephan into leaning over the drain as I blow into the tube from below. This results in much yelling at me.

DAY 21

Beautiful blue day, mid-sixties, and the inevitable could no longer be put off: it's gonna be a long cold winter, and we need firewood. First we had to drag all sorts of old, dead, and rotting stuff away from the trail I cut years ago.

(I was lazy and kind of just pushed everything out of the way, so the trail has been more like an impenetrable tunnel and we could not drag newly cut wood onto it.) There are lots of dead standing trees along the trail, and we cut those first. And that's when we found a much older trail, perfectly straight, broad, and in need of only minor clearing. *It comes within five feet of my twisting trail, ARGH!* We all agreed to pretend we had not seen it, and to this day we have never walked its length.

Sweaty work with the chain saw, but a good reason for us all to go swimming off the rocks before cocktail hour, in beautiful clear Bahama-like water. We're in bed by seven.

DAY 25

Because it's real windy today and the batteries are overcharging, Wendy can use her new Dustbuster vacuum. This really makes her happy, seems to rank up there with chocolate and sex.

DAY 26

Our woodpile is growing. It is difficult to know just how much wood we will need for the winter, our previous experience in this category being back in Idaho, when we would argue over whether to keep the thermostat at sixty or sixty-five degrees. On our next trip ashore I phone my friend Martin, who tells me, "Seven cords of hardwood, you're gonna have to get it brought out. You can't burn that spruce. And you gotta buy it dry, or you guys will freeze to death." And I remember why he is such a good friend: like me, not knowing anything about a particular thing only encourages him to say more about it, perhaps speak a little louder and quicker. I ask to speak to his wife, Marilyn, and she assures me that he has never lived in a house with a woodstove and that as far as she knows he doesn't even know where the furnace in their home is—that's her department—and that they often argue about whether to keep their thermostat at sixty-five or seventy degrees.

As we are loading groceries into the boat on the mainland, I ask Junior about the wood. "By Jeezus, start cutting now—I'm already doing next year's." So, with this encouragement we return to our island, where *whatever wood we cut will be exactly the amount of wood we need, says me. It's my island, DAMNIT!* (And isn't that the point of owning an island anyway?)

The dogs are in total bliss. They wait for us on the rocks when we go off in the boat, and no matter how long we've been gone, they are there to jump in the water to meet us, getting pretty much everything at least a little wet. They are perfect dogs.

Strange peanut-sauce-over-vegetables dinner, with rice and rotting leftover coleslaw. Rain in the evening. Our water tanks finally begin to fill.

Wendy
I've been really emotional lately, but Daniel makes it okay for me to be just me, tears and all. I love him.

I am getting very sick of carrying big logs to the house. I liked it better when I just had to turn up the thermostat. Firewood is heavy, and we have a lot more to cut and carry.

DAY 27—AUGUST

Fiercely clear morning. On the VHF marine radio gossip channel the news update is that Sylvester Stallone was in nearby Carleton on his seven- or twenty-six-million-dollar 125- or 225-foot yacht, depending on who you talk to. A big yacht does go by and I stagger around for much of the morning crying, *"I love you, Adrian!"*

Then comes the mammoth woodstove trek of the century. Our old woodstove was a converted fifty-five-gallon drum. Junior accurately named it the "you'll havta get outta there twice" stove and, sure enough, the first and every other time we lit the monster it got too hot to stay anywhere inside and we'd all run out to cool off, go back in, and then run out again! It would have heated a barn. So we gave in and ordered a smaller cast-iron thing with a nice glass front. It was delivered to Junior's dock today, and the beast seems to weigh eleven tons. We strapped two six-foot-long two-by-fours onto it and could just lift it, sort of how servants would carry royalty. I was in front, Wendy and Stephan each holding one board in the rear. We trudged, fell, laughed, grunted, and complained. Whenever we stood still the weight of our load made us sink into the mossy trail. Of course we were also dribbling the dogs like soccer balls. Amazingly we carried it, just the three of us. Stephan is growing into a strong boy, and just in time. I was proud—this was the single heaviest thing carried to our home, and we did it, just family.

Next we need a way to keep the floor from catching fire. We put on three backpacks and hike to the far side of the island. On Pebble Beach we collect fist-sized round and egg-shaped stones, each an ancient story told only with geological patience. We load up as many as we can, helping one another put on the packs. With much moaning, groaning, complaining, and laughing, we carry and stumble the rocks home. I screw a simple two-by-four wood frame into the floor around the stove. We spill the rocks within the framework and stand back, a little surprised at how perfectly they fill the area. Also at how beautiful it looks, the black speckles of mica matching the black of the stove.

DAY 29

Stephan and I moved the windmill today. We rigged a mastlike pipe to a tree and ran two hundred feet of heavy and expensive No. 4 wire to the house. Stephan buried the parts of it that cross the trail and our "yard." Naturally he also buried parts of himself. He called me over, where I found him apparently without legs. Needless to say, it took a while to get him extricated. I then connected wires to the batteries with only one explosion of sparks (which blew off a dime-sized chunk of the butter knife I was using as a screwdriver). We can no longer feel it turning, but we sure can hear it. I like to watch it, and think I'm the one making electricity.

We also set up the bathroom roof to collect the rain-water that spills over from the main roof. We now have about 550 square feet of roof collecting all the water we will need. I love to sit by the two fifty-five-gallon tanks on the first floor and listen to the water pour in. It is sooth-ing, like watching a fire.

Wendy, Stephan, and I can get the dogs to howl. First off the mood must be right—you can't just go at it dur-ing a meal, or at sleep time. It also cannot be too hot. I begin barking, throwing in a yelp now and then. The dogs perk their ears—more than that really; they focus their whole beings with an intensity I envy. Next, Wendy and Stephen chime in, the tone escalating in yips and yelps. Then Bear joins in with a few tentative barks, Abby contributing with a sort of loud whining sound similar to a bag of hamsters being run over by a go-cart. The time is right, and with an instinct that just won't go away, we all break into the howl together. Bear's shoulders hunch and the hairs on his back stand up. Even Abby, bred for generations of . . . um, something, even she can do it, though a little squeakily. It is a happy moment in our lives and usually disintegrates in laughter and general tail wag-ging. We all feel better, uplifted and released.

DAY 30

These bizarre laughing birds were around again last night. They give a sort of giggle-hiccup animal chirp, a squeaky hinge crying out for oil. You feel somehow em-barrassed when you hear them, like they have caught you in the act of doing something private. Since I hear them only when I'm peeing off the porch in the middle of the night, I can't help but take it personally. I call them denial birds because I automatically deny whatever they are saying about me.

DAY 33

Long day: we cut and haul wood. In the afternoon Stephan goes swimming in the harbor.

DAY 35

August is warm and amiable. I am tempted to relax, not worry about all the preparations for winter.

Wendy and I spend sunrise watching a cormorant get repeatedly stuck in the trees just beneath our windows. Cormorants are web-footed seabirds that should have no business being in trees. This guy lands by crashing into a treetop, which bends to absorb his impact and then spring-launches him ass first back in the direction he came from, into another tree. For five minutes he doesn't move, draped like a flung-at-the-wall-to-see-if-it's-done piece of spaghetti. Finally he looks around and then sort of trips into the air. He loses altitude fast (on water they have to "run" for quite a way to get airborne), and he scrunches around another tree, where he falls backward and, I swear to God, lies there on his back, barely balanced on a branch and looking dejectedly at heaven. We were about to launch a rescue party, bring him to the water, maybe give him a pep talk, but he finally mustered himself and flew off, probably too embarrassed to visit this island again. It's a pity the denial birds didn't see, because I would have liked to laugh with them for once.

DAY 36

Wendy

Daniel caught a little bird that was fluttering around us when we woke up this morning. I could see its heart beating; its whole chest shook.

―――

We wake up to a little brown bird fluttering around our heads. I gently catch it and release it outside. I pause and think: if the world blew up right now, I'd get caught with a *good* deed as my final act. That's not selfish of me, is it?

Going for karmic broke I dig a new pit for the outhouse (which is by the harbor and the fishing shack). Steph and Wendy dig the dirt out from around the wood beams under the main house so they won't rot. Then they begin to make a garden; they are a good team.

Abby can barely keep up with destroying it.

IT IS FOUR-THIRTY in the morning and I find myself on the couch, sleeping off some argument. I remember I was wrong, and didn't want to wait around to find out how much more wrong I could get, so I ran away—my standard defense—and am in the small shack by the harbor, sleeping alone. I'm putting into words the nasty feelings of *wanting to be single again, free of marriage demons, free to feel sorry for myself without the risk of getting caught being so stuck*. Do I just up the Prozac dose? But when I do that my soda's flat, and what's the point of breathing?

Sometimes I just cannot contain all the fireworks trying to bust out. Being in a marriage can feel like having surrendered. I think of my favorite Fitzgerald quote:

> Out of the corner of his eye Gatsby saw that the blocks of the sidewalk really formed a ladder and mounted to a secret place above the trees. He could climb to it, if he climbed alone, and once there he could suck on the pap of life, gulp down the incomparable milk of wonder.
>
> He knew that when he kissed this girl and forever wed his unutterable visions to her perishable breath, his mind would never romp again like the mind of God. So he waited, listening for a moment longer to the tuning-fork that had been struck upon a star. Then he kissed her.

DAY 37

I snuck back to the house early and made Wendy a cheese omelette.

Stephan

We hauled another ton of wood today. The stacks are getting larger and larger every day. The clouds are beautiful on the horizon.

4. Island Life

Every man looks at his wood-pile with a kind of
affection. I loved to have mine before my window,
and the more chips the better to remind me of my
pleasing work.

—THOREAU

DAY 38

Today Stephan is building a fort. We hear him hacking
with the machete and yelling, "Come see, come see!"
He's cut down hundreds of dead trees—each maybe ten
feet high and as thick as a wrist. These he has tied together into walls that enclose an area big enough for a
school bus. He's begging us to come and attack him.
Funny, knowing the most trouble he can get into is with
a machete is comforting. Living in this world is so much
safer; traffic and the Internet are to me greater worries.
(I see the Internet as the collective colostomy bag of our
culture, and I prefer Stephan poking out the eyeballs of
dead fish he finds washed up.)

The windmill is quiet in its new and sheltered location,
doing about six rpms while just a few feet above it

seagulls pant audibly to gain on the twenty-five-knot wind. It seems we set it up in a small windless zone— shit! Plan C next?

Stephan says he saw three ghosts by his fort today. "There was a man, a woman in her middle thirties wearing a hood, and a squirrel."

There is a story about a local ghost. A fisherman named Angus says she was killed by an angry man from Weed Harbor. He says she floats around and does no harm except for "scaring the piss out of me and my brothers late at night."

I don't believe in bad ghosts, just unhappy ones.

I had heard rumors of ghosts and gold on Whale Island. I followed them to Peter's wife's father, Russell Clayton, who talked to me three weeks before he died.

"Well now," he began, leaning against Junior's boatshed, "this is my father's story. He'd be one hundred and twenty-one, if he were living. So it was his grandfather's father, it happened then, over two hundred years ago.

"This is what happened.

"There was a square rigger, and she went ashore, on Whale Island. It was in the winter. And it was very cold, a lot of snow. . . . It was an awful storm, where she went at. . . . She smashed up quite fast. . . .

"So, she had a lot of gold aboard.

"Now, these people on the ship took the gold, and they divided it up amongst themselves. . . . And three of them built something, and they got across the narrows, and they left for Carleton. And it took them quite a while.

"It took three weeks to get back to 'um on the island, and they were all froze to death. It was very, very hard winters in them days, and you know what it's like when a southerly comes in and them big seas come rolling in on them rocks . . . and the gold was buried . . . and this is how the story went."

The story continues. Within the last fifty years two families have lived on Whale Island during the summers, and they were hardworking fishermen. I don't know if this was just men or whole families, if they owned the island or were squatters, but the story goes that both families left Whale Island suddenly. One even left all their lobster pots on the shore. That is like someone whose life savings are invested in his business—in a crane, for example—moving away without the crane. Rumor has it this family moved to the United States, bought a home, and retired. Did they find the gold? No one will say, but everyone loves to speculate.

I am happy to share this island with any spirits. I am looking forward to meeting them.

DAY 40

Grueling hard work wood-hauling day! By our calculations, with an average log at 18 inches and a pile of wood 3.5 by 64 feet, we have 336 cubic feet of wood. Since 8 feet by 4 by 4, or one cord, is 128 cubic feet, *we now have two and a half cords!*

It has not rained enough to fill our tanks, and the water sources we've been scrounging from are almost dry now.

In the trees by his fort, Stephan found a good seep—a small well—and we're nursing that, using buckets to scoop out the water. We inadvertently collect some sediment with it, which clogs the foot pump, but I joke that the floaties count as supplemental vegetables and are a good source of fiber. Plus I get to go outside to blow up the drain pretty regularly, with a good chance of being able to get someone wet even if they are sitting five feet away.

Clam chowder, brilliant clear sunset, and ships floating along the horizon.

DAY 42

Red and foggy sunrise. Wendy is oiling our floor while listening to one of my favorite Partridge Family CDs. We're sipping awful instant coffee. I'm singing along, not missing a word, and thinking how lucky I am to have a girl I can sing Keith Partridge tunes to.

Wendy

I took a solar shower today that Daniel set up for me. There was so much gunk floating in the water that I cried and yelled at him to fix it. Tomorrow we are going into town to go shopping and do laundry. Daniel has begun storing extra food for the winter. He says we may not get ashore for weeks at a time then.

• • •

DAY 46

With the island's water supply almost depleted we go ashore to buy some jugs of bottled water. I hate giving in to this. We drive an hour and a half to Galeville and decide to spend the night at a hotel. Stephan is glued to the TV and can't be bothered with meals. I think of the money we're saving on food. Wendy and I spend hours in the bathtub. Anyone who has roughed it knows the bliss of a long hot bath. I remember returning from my year at sea in my small sailboat. The first night ashore, in a single bath, I used two month's worth of water.

In town a little boy walks behind his mother. He is trying to drink a two-handed soda through a straw and he is having trouble. He has not yet learned to do two things at once. He doesn't know how to let anything happen without paying serious attention. He can't work a task with only half his being. Each sip causes his legs to slow down, provoking a "Hurry up" from Mom. He releases the straw, picks up speed, but then remembers he's got a soda in his hands, and the thirsty cycle begins again. I watch three repetitions before they are out of sight.

DAY 47

Stephan

Very wet and cold boat ride back to the island. I was scared.

~~~~

It was a crushing return to the island for Wendy, who's trying so hard to beautify this place, turn it into a home.

First, the oil she carefully applied to the floor before we left has dried in small semichunky puddles. Next, the cabinet she had specially built doesn't fit against the wall because of how the wall is leaning. The stained-glass "art" we carefully carried out not only broke in two places, it clearly would not have fit in anyway. All this triggers memories of failure and she sighs, sitting down in one of the two "Well, they looked good in the store" chairs. I try to comfort her and mumble, "Don't worry, honey, it's not like anyone will ever have to see this place."

On the bright side of things the rain barrels are finally full, 110 gallons. But of course we just bought and carried out a hundred dollars' worth of fancy bottled spring water. This is about a third of the evidence I've gathered in this lifetime to prove that God has a sense of humor.

DAY 51

I took Wendy out in the boat; I want her to be able to handle it in case I get hurt. Given how the lesson went, I must now believe in my own invincibility. When she was at the helm I could not help myself from saying things like "Er, hon, I've never seen barnacles that big *dead ahead!*" or "Did you see that snail pass us?"

Is this what's called codependent, where you secretly don't want your partner to get better at anything because then they will realize that you are not necessary for them?

Sometimes when I am feeling low I think of this woman who loves me. There must be something good in me to be loved by her. She is too smart and heart-wise to have been tricked.

The remains of hurricane somebody or other are heading this way. Only some wind and rain are expected, but any storm excites me. I long for an excuse worthy of my not having to be in control, and if that means a hurricane, so be it.

DAY 53

Windy night—I'm guessing there were forty-knot gusts. The windmill *shook* the house. It sounded like a power saw just outside the window. The voltage was hitting 16.2, several volts past cooking. From now on I must tie the windmill blades down before a storm; they move too quickly to catch during a storm. Big seas are washing over many rocks that I've never even seen wet. There is a natural blowhole we can watch spouting fifty-foot spurts when a wave hits right. The water comes in under a ledge and then spouts up from a crack in what looks like a whale's back. We call it "Moby Dicking."

DAY 54

Ferocious day of woodcutting. According to my calculations, we have 619 cubic feet of moist blue spruce, which comes to over four and three-quarter cords, short one pile of our five-cord goal. When I explain this to Wendy, she yells, "That's it, I will never carry another piece of wood in my life, I am so fucking done!"

So, having taken everything into careful consideration . . . we are officially done. I figure it took us about twenty-six days to cut, haul, and stack a winter's worth of wood. (A week later Junior sees our woodpile and I ask him what he thinks. I get the Nova Scotian equivalent of a New Yorker's shrug. The translation: "Eh, it could be worse.")

We ate crabs for dinner, small ones Stephan collected from the harbor. "Oh please, can't we eat these? I caught twenty-two, please?" After trying to eat just one Wendy says, "Well, I guess *that's* why we've never seen these at the market." For dessert Stephan grosses us out with a discussion about their eyeballs, which he says were especially chewy. We play gin rummy for an hour before a deep night's sleep.

DAY 59—SEPTEMBER
Stephan
Daniel and I went fishing today. We caught our own dinner. Mom made killer cookies.

———

When I first met Stephan I was nervous with the same excitement I experience at a palm reading. Six-year-olds are still relatively new to the world, and have not paid too much attention to all the warning signs of life that their parents have imposed on them. Their souls are still very much awake, and I somehow fear that these beings, closer to God than I, will see through me and laugh. But I was ready that day; a twelve-day-old puppy was in my jacket pocket.

I had just picked up my new dog, Godzilla, whose mother had been killed by a car. I was feeding him with an eye dropper. His eyes were barely open. He was the newest of beings and every one of his breaths seemed conscious; he was only just learning his body.

Wendy pointed to a child crawling under some picnic tables. This was at a shared friend's wedding, and Wendy's husband was somewhere else. I crawled under the table. "I'm Daniel," I said, holding out my dog. "Wow, that looks like a Bear," said Stephan. "Can I hold him?" And thus, with some distraction, our first meeting was on, and Bear had been properly named. I think the puppy magically allowed me to be simple and enjoy Stephan as the gift that he was, not so different from the puppy really. I kind of envied that.

Stephan's only suit was slowly shredding as we wandered under all the tables. He was a little rounder than most kids, had messy blond hair and eyes like his mother, ocean blue. He was mostly smile, his face revealing his excitement, his joy.

Wendy's eyes are big and blue. She has dirty-blond hair and is built like my sailboat, ready for any seas. We both worked at the same wilderness school for wild teenagers. I worked out "in the field"; she worked in the office. Wendy was very much a local girl, pregnant and married before graduating high school. Having grown up a liberal East Coast city boy, the idea of being married at eighteen, with child and debt, was new to me.

Wendy worked with six therapists for three years before suspecting that something was wrong in her marriage, that she had the right to not accept what she believed to be God's plan for her. Her life began to have an independent meaning as her coworkers spoke of her value, her skills, how her laugh lit up others' hearts, and how her warmth became the keystone on which our office thrived. Wendy began thinking that maybe God had intended for her to be a verb in her own life.

I took Wendy out to dinner near the end of this marriage. We had Mexican food and a beer. We talked, and she was miserable. At work she had always put up a front of the happy wife—that being part of what she "had to bear."

I encouraged her to get out, and not because I was there for her. I was still in my own adolescent search for the woman of my dreams, and Wendy, with a child, was not even a remote possibility.

I did, however, wonder what being in a family with a child and Wendy would be like. I immediately experienced the fear Sartre describes in walking by a cliff's edge: not so much that I might fall but that I was free to jump. That something in me wanted all these things, craved some sort of stability in a manic life.

I began to love Wendy as she began using the word "divorce" in nearly complete sentences. I saw a little girl waking up, questioning her life, and not, as I feared for myself, trying to become the perfect résumé. I began making a lot of extra Xeroxes, losing pens, needing paper clips, and thinking up any other excuse I could to be around her. I felt like a goofy sixteen-year-old. One night after her separation I watched her sleep. It was our first night, and it was intense to me, somehow shaking the foundations of what had become a fairly lighthearted activity for me. All night I gently touched her, felt her heart beating, her softness. Her soul seemed to hover where my hands caressed, and my own soul stirred in a new way, something different than the familiar gonging of lust.

During my first baby-sitting session with Stephan, we went food shopping. Their cupboards were quite bare: some cereal, pepper, milk, and a can of tuna fish. Stephan and I had a great adventure in the supermarket buying a cart full of groceries, Stephan sitting in the cart and laughing while slowly being buried in food. The only rule was that sugar could not be the first, second, or third ingredient of anything he put into the cart. I got my first taste of how thorough a small kid can be, as he read almost all the junk-food labels in the store in his quest for sweets.

We filled the cupboards, we filled the fridge, and food overflowed onto the countertops. When Wendy got home from work she cried—I thought out of happiness, but it was really out of fear that she would have to cook, something she had been forced to do and hated. So Stephan and I made a huge lasagna, and Stephan stepped in it only once when it was briefly on the floor. (Note: A lasagna noodle is fully cooked when it adheres to a child's foot or leg.) The meal was great, and then I helped Stephan with his piano lesson, and the night was long and wonderful.

Two years later I asked Stephan if I could marry his mom, before I'd asked her. It was obvious to me that his approval would be required, that he was part of the deal. He quickly said, "Yes, you make my mom happy." I had money then and bought her a big diamond ring, and I asked her, and she cried, and I cried too.

DAY 60
Wendy

What an incredible sunrise. I was looking out at the ocean and suddenly saw the very first part of the sun come up over the horizon. I watched the whole thing happen, and it was beautiful. I've never been quiet enough to watch the whole thing before.

It feels like the beginning of fall. I could see my breath in the air this morning. The leaves are falling off the only trees here that are not spruce.

―――

For the nine years that I've owned this island there has been no dock. What we've done is unload the boat on the beach or rocks, depending on the tide. Then with an easily tangled jumble of rope and two pulleys, we haul the boat out to a big anchor, and there she waits, midharbor. . . . Over the years I've occasionally had to swim out to deweed the pulleys, and this water is never warm, since we're only some one hundred miles south of the icebergs' home territory. With winter and its big storms and ice, the awareness I must maintain about any boat in the water will cause an aneurysm, so *it is time for our own dock!*

There is a pile of rocks on the beach in our harbor. The rocks are all about as big as one person can pick up, maybe two hundred of them; this is where an old dock once stood. Around here docks are not the elegant New England treated-lumber-planked affairs that I grew up seeing. Here you can do one of two things. You can build a box big enough to hold a Volkswagen out of scrap lumber. Maybe it is made out of stuff that washed ashore, or maybe from trees you cut from your backyard. You secure this box to the bottom by filling it with rocks. After at least two of these are built—one in deeper water than the other—you then plank over and connect them with straight whole trees of whatever thickness you want. This is the sort of dock Junior and his boys built, and the sort that ends up as a pile of rocks in your harbor after a really big storm. The second local dock type is a slipway resembling a strip of railroad track turned over, with the railroad ties resting on long logs bolted to the biggest rocks available. You do this on a sloping shore, extending from minimum low tide up to above storm high tide at an angle shallow enough to haul out on.

The pile of rocks here are from the first type of dock, last rebuilt maybe fifty years ago by a family that lived and fished here. This sort of dock offers a lot of resistance to the ocean, especially to winter ice, and is better suited for a sheltered area. Our small harbor is terrific in all but the biggest storms, but those are exactly what you have to build for; whether it's a yearly or fifty-year storm doesn't matter—it could start in twenty minutes. A slipway will be better here, so I scheme until I have a sufficient mental picture to work with. I'm so excited that I almost draw a plan, but then decide on no plan. I like being creative in the moment, and a plan scares me.

ABBY'S FAVORITE GAME in life is to convince Bear that *she's right*. She'll bark, changing tones and facing a new direction and perking her ears just so—and Bear will ignore her until she hits a new note and some special act of dire attention, and then he'll become *convinced* that something is there, and so they'll both bark. She becomes thrilled that he's paying her attention . . . then there is a pause and it begins again.

DAY 61

Stephan

I saw Mom and Daniel having sex. Great pancakes for breakfast. We played horseshoes today.

DAY 62

It was a blowy night. The house trembled and it was as if we'd put a quarter in the slot of a vibrating hotel bed. It was a board-game sort of morning, so we had Monopoly with our coffee, followed by some baseball excitement on the lawn. We listened to radio reports of a crashed airplane off Halifax, 219 dead. We can hear the various rescue ships searching for debris on our VHF radio. I wonder about what went through 219 people's minds as they were going down, what wishes, fears, regrets. It is the part of life that most interests me, the it-all-boils-down-to-these-last-moments part.

I've lived those moments of peeking at death several times: in a small sailboat on a big ocean in a storm, clinging to a rock cliff fifty feet above the ground, and once accidentally shooting myself and waiting in stunned silence for blood or pain to tell me where the bullet had gone in. All three times I was overwhelmed with a sadness that here I was about to die and I couldn't share the experience with another, that I would have to do it alone.

I recently took out a million-dollar life-insurance policy so that my last moments do not include any guilt about not providing for Wendy and Stephan. I tell Wendy, "Sure, it would suck, but you'd be able to get a new car!" I also took out a quarter-million-dollar policy on Wendy because I've always wanted a Humvee, and before we were married I actually had the money in the bank for one. So if I ever do become a bachelor again, it will be with a Hummer, and I've promised to get vanity plates that read: WENDY.

5. Acorns and Visitors

> He was so genuine and unsophisticated that no
> introduction would serve to introduce him, more than
> if you introduced a woodchuck to your neighbor.
>
> —THOREAU

DAY 63—VISITORS

Peter has come to visit a few times, but today he brings his oldest friend, Aaron. When the seas are calm you can come right up to the house. They show up near sunset, anchoring their big boat close and rowing their skiff ashore. "Duck-hunting season starts tomorrow," says Peter, "and *we already got two.*"

This is a great time for these guys; good old hunting and gathering is hard to beat for making a guy feel good. During each short legal fishing season—lobster, mackerel, sea urchin, snow crab, or scallop—they work long, long hours. Not until their off weeks—or even months, due to storms—can they relax and booze it up. So for brief periods of the year there is a lot of drinking. They arrive already drunk.

My family often hides when Peter shows up. Sometimes Stephan peers at us, wanting to be a part of something not available from his mother, and I am guilty of not seeing or hearing him, for he is small and Peter can be huge.

We have more than a few beers. We tell stories, we exaggerate, we lie, confess, curse, and make promises. We speak of our dreams. We do what men seem to have to do: we share our isolation and for a few moments are completely known.

The trails on the island can barely contain us. I watch Peter go diagonal and thrash through the trail's edge, where a tree catches and holds him up, springing him back onto the trail.

When he and Aaron leave, the whole island is silent. Wendy and Stephan reappear. "Wow" is about all any of us can say.

DAY 64

Quack, *boom, POP!* and hunting season is on. As the sun rises it's raining ducks around Aaron and Peter's boat. I see some other boats to the east, but I'm rooting for the ducks anyway. Which does not prevent me from accepting two from Peter. Feast! Sauté in garlic, apples, soy sauce, sugar, and onions.

Wendy

I'm glad Daniel is the cook in this family. If it were me, we would all starve. I'm good at breakfast—Daniel wakes up every morning saying, "Where the hell is my coffee?" as he snuggles next to me. Stephan's favorite is French toast. He begs me to make this often.

I have learned to make homemade bread, and boy am I good at it. I can make challah and an awesome rye bread. This is definitely a main staple for us. (We also could not live without my chocolate-chip cookies.)

I have an oven board I bought at an antique store, and Daniel hooked it up so that it hinges down and up. I can put it up while I'm chopping vegetables or kneading bread and then put it back down for more room when I'm through using it. The propane stove/oven is just big enough to fit one round loaf of challah. The trick is making sure the propane tank doesn't run out before the bread's done.

DAY 65

Rainy foggy morning. We get up early to go ashore. It's still stormy, and as we wake we watch spray blow over the rocks a hundred feet to mist our windows. We wear our float suits for the first time, heavy neoprene full-body life jackets. They are bulky but wonderfully snug, like a turtle's shell. I drop Wendy and Stephan ashore for laundry and food shopping. They love to be together; Stephan can soak in her love without any competition from me.

IT FASCINATES ME how we consider ourselves superior to the other creatures on our planet. That we have somehow risen above our brutal past existence as hunters and gatherers is, well, just bullshit. Our lives are hardly different from those of our ancestors, and I am happy when I am caught in any embarrassing animalistic behavior.

Food, for example. I'm a squirrel, a paranoid squirrel who lives in constant fear of the first snow. Do I have enough acorns hidden for Whale Island's eternal winter? Where did I hide them anyway?

We now have enough food for several months. My favorite are the military's MREs (meals, ready to eat). MREs have a shelf life of at least five years. They come in a heavy plastic bag, about as big as one of your feet, and inside is everything you could want, including salt, pepper, sugar, coffee, gum, toilet paper, matches, a spoon, Tabasco sauce, and a moist towelette. Each of the food items is separately sealed in a you-can-get-into-it-only-if-you-are-really-hungry plastic-and-foil pouch. This includes a main course of perhaps chicken tetrazzini, some applesauce, a powdered sugar drink, crackers with jelly, cheese, or peanut butter, and a dessert like a chocolate cookie. Some MREs even include a "self-heat" pouch. You simply pour a quarter cup of water in the pouch, put your food pack in, and stand back. They hardly ever explode, and three minutes later you've got a hot meal that some people say tastes like cat food, but I love it for its convenience and calories. Hairballs aren't so bad anyway.

The best part of an MRE is the labeling. Army people, or at least the ones who do the labeling, seem to have exceptionally low IQs. The self-heat pouch says DO NOT EAT. The drink package exclaims BEVERAGE BASE, POWDER, APPLE CIDER. Another proclaims its contents as JAM,

STRAWBERRY, and sometimes you get one with the coded message 8 2 8 5 5 1 3 2; I have no idea what it means, but to me it tastes great.

On those days when I find myself humming the Rolling Stones' tune "Mother's Little Helper," there ain't nothing like an MRE!

Besides the MREs our diet is what I would call pretty normal. Fresh meats don't last long, so we have them only on the night we return from the mainland. Tomatoes do not take well to the trip, nor do bananas. Between the grocery store and our kitchen everything must be picked up and handled six times: from shopping cart to car, to the dock, handed into the boat, carried from the boat and left on the rocks at our landing, and then carried a quarter of a mile over the twisting root-tripping trail.

Thank goodness for cans! Under the couch I built is a vast drawer—actually it's a plastic fisherman's bait box that washed ashore in '94—and it is full of cans. Behind it, a belly crawl farther, are an additional five rows of jars of peanut butter, jellies, and other staples.

Vegetables keep a lot better than people suspect. Onions and cabbage are perfectly fresh even after a month if kept halfway cool. An onion makes any meal taste good. (Well, almost. Not breakfast cereal.) Potatoes, apples, and oranges all last if not in the sun and not too badly banged up on the way out. We use canned milk for our coffee. We miss nothing, except maybe fried clams. We're all gaining weight, maybe because food is now a pleasure for us. We eat no meals on the run or standing up. We digest our food long enough to satisfy any grand-parent. Wendy cooks our bread, I continue my lifelong quest to discover something new (a combination like chocolate and peanut butter—something that will be named after me), and Stephan, well, he eats.

6. Married Life

The greater part of what my neighbors call good
I believe in my soul to be bad, and if I repent of
anything, it is very likely to be my good behavior.
What demon possessed me that I behaved so well?

— THOREAU

DAY 66

Wendy and Stephan have gone to Halifax for the night.
I think she wants to go shopping in the kind of stores
where the aroma knocks me over.

I had my first day all alone on the island and loved it,
guiltless. At night it really rained, and the brilliant rain-
water-overflow system that I'd developed had a problem,
namely that the water didn't flow down the pipe it was
supposed to. Luckily, just yesterday I completed creating
(my first) refrigerator. I cut a hole through the downstairs
floor and dug into the newly revealed dirt under the
house (finding a favorite hammer lost when the floor was
built). Then I buried one of those big Tupperware-esque
bins and carefully reassembled the cut-out floor. Picturing
a cherry on top of a banana split, I put a brass latch/toe
stubber in the center so I could pry the thing open. Any-

way, all unsupervised water, whether from the leaky roof or spilling over the brim of the rainwater barrel, finds its way and collects in this gravitational mecca.

It is possible that a trap-door refrigerator at the lowest point in a house that often has liquids such as rainwater or borscht running inside of it is not a good idea. Oh well; failure is an unnecessary deterrent for the ignorant. . . . I was able to fill an additional forty gallons of spare water tanks, so now we have 150 gallons, not counting what's in the fridge.

I am loving my day of bachelordom. The house is such a cozy mess, and there are no standards to adhere to. I have sauerkraut, Pringles, and mustard for lunch. I enjoy eating dropped morsels off the floor (if I get there before the dogs), and I can leave half my face unshaved.

Peter comes by at sunset. We sit on the rocks passing a bottle and feeling wonderfully free.

Wendy

I first met Daniel when I started my new job. I kept hearing everybody talk about this guy who was building a house on his island and how great he was. He walked into the office a couple of weeks later with the top of his nose bleeding because the hatch door on his pickup fell down on it. I thought to myself, This guy is supposed to be smart?

DAY 67

Ashore at five to get the girl, boy, and a small wooden skiff that Junior built during the winter. He has built one

each winter for the past twenty-eight. Beautiful shape—
she dances over the water like a Jesus bug. She is painted
dark green. I hope Stephan falls in love with her; every
rowboat needs a boy.

What can you do with a woman who buys *sod* for an
island in the North Atlantic? Wendy also has bought two
small birch trees, another thing that has never survived
this climate. But I don't even get to vocalize this thought,
as Abby eats all the leaves off both trees while we are carrying the sod to the house.

DAY 68

September eighth, our first official day of school. We rise
early, nine-thirty, and as Wendy hammers away on the
porch, Stephan and I hunch over some graph paper and
zing, off we go. We eat fresh blueberry muffins to sustain
ourselves through the rigorous activity of making the
one-to-twelve multiplication table. Stephan slows a little
when he gets to the sevens and eights. I get completely
lost there.

DAY 69

I try to tell Wendy that I don't think the sod she bought
will grow. She goes outside before I can finish. I follow,
and watch her unrolling and stomping on each row defensively. Now we have a five-row lawn. Then she goes
back inside to eat a whole bag of Nestlé's chocolate chips.
Her look dares me to say anything.

Later on she says, "Hey, what the hell happened to the

76

fridge, how'd all this water get in here?" Relying on eighteen years of overeducation to get me out of this one, I nimbly reply, "Uh, I dunno."

DAY 70

Stephan

Today I found a really big lobster pot with four huge lobsters. I fell overboard rescuing it. Its buoy was gone, so I had to grab the rope. Then we stripped the bark off the trees Daniel cut down so that we could make a dock for the boat. I fell in twice. I also caught five fish for dinner.

DAY 71

The dock construction is going on full speed. Last week we rented a generator and a massive rock drill. It's a pain in the ass to lug around, but the three-foot-tall drill makes a hole one inch wide by eight inches deep in three minutes, in solid granite. I drilled extra holes in a few prominent rocks; maybe they'll be useful later. After all twelve holes were filled with sixteen-inch stainless steel threaded bolts and cement that expands as it dries, we drilled through the trees we had cut. We bolted and nailed the whole mess together. Then we laid eight-foot logs across the "runners," and I don't think I've ever been prouder of anything I've made, including the salad bowl in third grade. There is something special about designing and building a thing from the ground up. Usually my dad helps—whatever he builds succeeds with elegance, so I am eager to step aside for the benefit of the project—but this scrounged bizarre tangle of timber is all ours: the idea, the labor, the mistakes, and the comedy. Perhaps this is yet another step into manhood, where I am the creator and my father is there only to smile upon my finished work. And just maybe Stephan will one day appreciate something about my style, and he'll be heartened by doing things his own way, and passing that along.

By dusk I'm slathered with sap. Our showers here are critical to maintaining a sense of comfort. "Hardships" are not so tough to endure when you are clean. Until recently we have been using a solar shower: basically just a thick-skinned black rubber three-gallon bag (French army surplus, $10). This absorbs sunlight while lying on a rock. It warms up nicely in about three hours. When the water feels right we hang it from a nail over our heads on the outside of the house. Gravity feeds the warm water through a spigot, and if you are quick, or shut it off and on between rinses, it works great. Wendy and I share one bag. Because Stephan only showers when forced—once a week—we let him use a whole bag. Of course on rainy days we stay dirty, as the water needs direct sunshine to heat up.

Last week I finished our indoor system, and it is as luxurious as the Plaza. First we heat up a three-gallon bucket of water on the propane stove. It takes only about six minutes to get warm. Hidden under the dining room table is an old water jug attached to the floor. With a funnel, we pour the heated water through a hole in our table and into the jug. A hose goes through the floor from the jug and connects to a spigot on the first floor. My father gave Wendy an ancient-looking bathtub he found at a junkyard, and we hung a shower curtain around it, suspended from the ceiling. The hose hangs over our heads with a little shower spigot attached. Except for the fact that the tub is by the foot of Stephan's bed, which sometimes gets wet, the whole thing is great. Three gallons runs for about four minutes, so we move fast. There is also a clamp behind the spigot, to control the flow. The tub drains through another hose that goes through the floor and into the dirt under the house, and yes, it's fun to blow in the end of that and scare whoever is in the shower.

DAY 72—LOBSTERS

Today is September twelfth, Landing Day, the final day of lobster season, when everyone must put up all 250 of their traps for the year. It's a day of hard work, and you can almost hear an audible collective sigh. For two months these guys have been busting butt, the money they make from their catch directly proportional to how vigilant they are. This money will be most of what they earn this year, and two months is a fairly short period of time. Peter has asked me to come along and help.

The alarm wakes me at four-thirty. I make a little noise getting ready, just enough so Wendy will think I am awfully manly getting up so early. I stumble to the slipway in the dark and rain. The weather is intrusive, the cold and wet immediately going to my skin. I push the boat down the almost completed ramp and happily start the engine, loving how I can operate still mostly asleep. By five o'clock I'm at Peter's wharf, tied up and just in time to meet him and Aaron as they stumble out of the camp. We pile into the *Defiance* and head out of the tiny cove. I could jump off and land dry on the rocks we skim past. The wind is gusting at over twenty knots from the southwest.

It is clear to me right away that I am little more than extra body weight. Working together all summer, Peter and Aaron are like the gears inside a well-oiled watch. Peter steers the *Defiance* next to the lobster-pot buoy, and Aaron snags the floating line with his gaff, hauls in, then throws the gaff onto the deck behind him with his right hand while handing the rope to Peter with his left hand. Peter drapes the line over the winch with his right hand while momentarily letting go of the wheel and with his left hand starts the hydraulics that spin the winch that pulls in the line. The lobster pot comes whizzing toward the surface, at first a dark and mysterious shape. Then Aaron drops the buoy in the boat as he neatly coils the fifty to one hundred feet of line. I help by untying the buoy. (A four-year-old could do it, but I hurry and grunt loudly, and make the most of it.) Peter maneuvers the pot on board so that it sits on a table directly between him and Aaron. Peter rapidly goes through the trap, throwing the small lobsters back, dropping the keepers in a bin, and tossing out any crabs or starfish. Usually he'll keep a fish, maybe a flounder, for the next meal. Aaron puts the coil of rope inside the trap, closes the pot, and while

Peter heads us for the next buoy, Aaron either hands it to me to stack or just keeps going with the boat's momentum and throws it himself onto the ever growing heap in the stern. All this in no more than a minute.

Between traps I go to the bin and put rubber bands on the lobsters claws. Since I have handled lobsters since I was a little kid, I am able to do this well enough to at least not get bitten.

During squalls the wind howls through us and our wet clothing. We stack the traps higher and higher, like bricks. The *Defiance* is big, and she holds eighty traps before there is absolutely no more room for us on board. Aaron throws a few more on top, and we head in toward Peter's camp.

At the beginning of this season two lobstermen had too many traps stacked in the stern of their boat. The wind was blowing strong and from behind them, and the traps became like a sail, so when they made the turn around Grubby Rock the wind caught them and rolled the boat right over. The traps were lost. Luckily they were being followed by another boat, and they somehow swam out from under and were quickly rescued. They were able to tow the boat back into Kingsland, upside down and minus its traps, very embarrassed. Later on the lobstermen hired Aaron to dive and recover most of the traps. These two guys were a lot luckier than they deserve. Aaron tells me, "What they did was ignorant, damn fools. Them's originally from Weed Harbor, you know" —just to remind me that no one from Kingsland could possibly be so foolish.

Peter brings the *Defiance* to the wharf, Aaron and I handling bow and stern lines. Peter begins tossing the traps onto the dock, and Aaron and I pick them up— Aaron two at a time—and carry them ashore and stack them six high. Getting traps five and six on top is difficult for me. I do it only when Aaron is immediately at hand to be impressed, testosterone supplying my needed strength.

With the first boatload ashore, we sit down for one of Peter's amazing breakfasts. Steak, bacon, eggs, potatoes, cold lobster, fried fish, and strong tea.

We make two more trips, busy until about four in the afternoon. We collect 120 pounds of lobster, three lobsters over ten pounds each. We also catch a three-foot catfish, which Peter says is good eating. I've never seen anything like it. It has fangs and an attitude.

By the end of the day, 247 traps are piled high in the grass by the wharf. Only three have been lost this year. (I'll find one of those washed up on our island a week later.) Some years a single storm may take a hundred traps.

My fingers are so swollen that I can barely work my zipper. Peter gives me three good-sized lobsters, and I head home happy that I have earned no more than my dinner.

DAY 73

Final work on the slipway now, and the big question is, Will it work? After years of insane projects I've learned not to assume that even gravity will work. Wendy and I boat ashore to take the winch off my truck. It's a heavy thing that inevitably falls on my foot. It runs on 12-volt, like everything else on the island, and it draws a lot of power—using it can stall my truck. So we also grab an extra 12-volt battery, and I'm proud to be enough of a redneck to have forty pounds of *extra battery* in my truck. Back on the island Stephan has finished building the two wide ladders we'll use to drag the boat over the sand at low tide. The slipway is about forty feet long, reaching the ocean only at midtide and higher. The sandy beach slopes evenly for another forty feet. The ladders, or "runners," hold the boat off the sand and can be placed end to end at low tides.

I carry, drop, and finally drag the winch to a boulder and secure it with cable to the steel eyebolt I put in last week. Stephan attaches jumper cables between the battery and the winch. Wendy clips the winch's cable into the boat's bow eye. I flip the switch, and with a slow grinding and an unusual electric sound, the boat reluctantly begins to move. Then I remember the grease. Stephan and I happily plunge our hands into a big tub of white slipperiness, and goo the stuff all over every piece of wood the boat might touch.

The fun begins with Stephan tricking me into looking down at *"something really gross!"* as he points to my shirt. His hand *fwaps* up, and I have a white grease beard. He shrieks in joy and runs off into the trees. I am frozen for a moment as a flood of memories wells up. This was my absolute favorite thing to do to my father.

Suddenly I am the victim and not the victor! I let out a Tarzan yell and try to pursue Stephan, only to slip on the *slipway,* crashing to the rocks with my usual raw-liver-like aplomb. When Stephan taunts from the forest, I am laughing too hard to get up.

Chaos follows: picture two slightly chubby humans pursuing one another and trying to smear globs of grease on each other. Add two hysterical dogs.

Eventually we run out of grease and calm down. Wendy stands about fifty feet away, ready to run off if either Stephan or I move in her direction. She returns only after supervising, in a strict voice, the cleanup. Finally I coax her back by offering her the honor of working the electric switch. Our small boat gently glides uphill until she's high and dry ten feet above the tides. Wendy cheers, I raise my arms in victory, and Stephan runs in circles until he slips on one of his ladders. The dogs don't seem especially impressed, but they enjoy our enthusiasm and are clearly happy. I set up one of our solar panels to charge the battery, because one long pull from low tide practically drains it. Another big job done.

DAY 74
Stephan has his first *phallic symbol* moment. After making sure Mom can't see, he holds up a tree he's carrying like a giant penis and whispers, "Daniel, look!" And then falls over giggling uncontrollably.

• • •

DAY 76

Right now is such a perfect moment. We're eating fresh-from-the-mail chocolate, the wind is north, and the water is sparkling. Wendy is reading some girl-furniture magazine, lost in a world of perfect window arrangements. Bear's on the landing farting. Abby is at my feet bleeding a little from when she attacked Wendy's machete. Again, it's not that she is *stupid* exactly, it's just that her mind has no RAM. If what needs to be thought of is not coincidentally already on the screen when it is needed, well then . . .

DAY 77

We're up at five-thirty and watch the sunrise. Ripples of red with orange ribbons and a big yellow ball. Wendy and I spoon, snuggle bliss.

Wendy and I may fight a lot, but it's usually only half serious. I think the ability to laugh at ourselves is what keeps us together.

DAY 78

Parts of Wendy's lawn blew away last night, and I can see sections snagged up on the woodpile.

Great walk around the island; collected rocks and finally visited the bog on the the north side of the island. It has grown up quite a bit since I fell in it years ago · · ·

Stephan is definitely absorbing some of my cynical mannerisms. Wendy is fastidiously neat, and she come upstairs to see Stephan "cooking." He has someho

exploded an egg—it's on his elbow, the counter, his shirt, and outlines where Bear was sitting. In a voice quivering with suppressed anger she asks, "Why is there egg all over?" to which Stephan instantly replies, "Bad genetic material?" I am secretly proud.

DAY 80

Do the planets actually align themselves in certain ways that cause shitty days for us on the earth? Today it seems so; we are all on edge. Even Abby gets smacked for biting Wendy on the ass. Bear and I get disgusted (as much at ourselves) and go for a green-boat ride around the island, making Wendy even more mad. Then I come back to do the upstairs porch and I just don't have any ideas what to do with it. It is six feet deep and runs along the ocean side of the house, just level with the treetops. A small door takes you out to it (another leaky spot just over Stephan's bunk). I want to figure out a way to build a table, deck, and chairs, some whale-vertebrae stools, a big piece of driftwood, and an elephant-tusk-shaped piece of tree I saved from the woodpile . . . but my muse has left the building, and I stand dumbly scratching myself. The only thing I feel good about right now is that after I threw one of the chairs into a tree, it stuck nicely, about ten feet off the ground. It looks like a tree-elf throne. This pisses Wendy off. She sees it as a mean comment on the style of chair she bought. I see it as the only art I am capable of today.

• • •

DAY 91—OCTOBER

Stephan

I got yelled at first thing in the morning. Today was a really bad day. At least we had borscht for lunch.

DAY 92

Wendy tells me that sometimes I don't treat Stephan as a son, and I cannot deny it. It's like I have no idea how to do that, or maybe just enough idea to know how lost I am at it. I assume it involves unconditional love. When Stephan gets angry it feels like there is hatred for me in his whole being. How can I love that?

When my dad got that angry, and he did, the whole family had to tiptoe around, and I hated being dominated that way, like none of my feelings were relevant. Here I am thirty years later, only it's not my dad but my kid! According to a psychic whose book I am reading, I must have designed this into my life for a very specific reason.

There is a Hitler in our midst, and it is me. Maybe regular parents have a whole support system I don't know about, but I don't. It's not natural.

Here are the simple things I do to earn my place ahead of Hitler in line for Judgment Day:

I don't let him eat chocolate for breakfast.

I ask him to pick up his clothes off the floor.

I make him do schoolwork.

I won't always play cards with him.

I don't make him macaroni and cheese after he doesn't eat what I already cooked him.

I ask him to chew with his mouth closed.

And about a hundred other things I suspect a well-adjusted mom or dad puts up with daily. Is it because they are so thrilled that what has sprung from their loins has progressed beyond the initial stage of resembling a zucchini? Yes, I imagine that is something to be proud of, but is that all that is required to initiate unconditional love, *that it used to look like a zucchini and my, my, look at the improvement!*

Or is my problem that I am going against the will of nature? Male lions do not tolerate stepchildren. The first thing a guy lion does after beating up the older boss is to kill any cubs. He is not about to waste his energy raising some other guy's DNA, so he kills the kids and then humps all the lady lions and thus fathers only his own.

Sometimes late at night I hear Steph nightmaring with grunts of "Okay, okay! . . . I know . . . I didn't!" and I know these are all the defenses he is building as a result of me. I remember how utterly miserable I was in sixth grade. I heard anything my father said to me as criticism. I could never be as perfect as he was. Stephan seems optimistic in comparison.

DAY 93

Clear sky (outside anyway). I did some waterproofing, Wendy painted chairs. I went for another island circle in the green boat with Bear. I stand amidships and can steer the 1.5-horsepowered dingy just by leaning. Bear stands forward like a happy hood ornament. Later Wendy makes whole-wheat bread and peanut-butter cookies. Then we play progressive rummy.

I think the key is that I lack the genetic disposition to allow Stephan to win at card games. The problem is that if I do begin winning, Stephan begins to sulk. His shoulders drop, he frowns, and every card he picks up is the wrong one. He gets into this mind-set where he really believes that God has dropped everything else on the planet so as to fully concentrate on making his life miserable. As any game that he is not winning progresses, his personal thundercloud darkens and rumbles. The air becomes electric. A storm is imminent.

Wendy plays into this, saying, "Oh, Stephan, it's just chance, anything can happen." I counter with, "No, honey, Stephan is convinced he'll lose. And lose he will."

I deal the next hand. Progressive rummy is a series of gin rummy–like hands where you keep score, and each new hand is progressively more difficult. When it's Stephan's turn, he doesn't want to discard.

"I can't decide, it isn't fair!"

"Stephan, you have to discard—pick one. Come on," Wendy says, trying to calm him.

"No, I don't have to. I can just take a penalty card instead!"

I say, "Stephan, I won't play with you if you make up rules as you go."

Stephan says, "My *dad* taught me, its true!" Naturally, mention of his father puts me at my emotional best, DEFCON 1.

"Great," I say. "I have a rule too. It's called you can't add a rule to the game when it happens to be really convenient. You have to wait till it does you no good before adding it!"

"Fine, I quit!!" He throws his cards at me. They flutter over my head like the first big raindrops.

"Stop it, both of you, just stop it!" Wendy says.

"You cheat, you always do this!" I say, my voice stony cold.

Stephan can yell quite loud when he wants to, and he wants to now. "NO, I DON'T! You always say that and it isn't true."

I'm shocked. This is not a simple "no" sort of event, but defiance, pure and simple. Why this causes me to launch all my missiles at once, I don't know. I feel like I'm in a Eugene O'Neill play, me the cranky bastard of a father being usurped by his children.

"Out. Get out. Now."

"No, I won't, I won't, I won't, I WONT!!!"

I cannot remember ever being angrier. It seems that my entire being has just been mocked, pointed at, and laughed at. By an eleven-year-old boy.

I jump up. Stephan stands defiantly. I reach around him, enclosing his arms, and squeeze him into a tight bear hug. I lean back until his feet are off the ground. I carry him toward the stairs, ready to carry him down and put him out the door.

Then something screams inside and I let him go. I back away from the stairs, from the abysmal darkness before me. What am I doing?

I breathe. Silence.

Something important has just happened, something that I know I will never forget. But whatever it was that had me, I stopped it.

I just stand there—horrified, numb, tingling, afraid. Stephan runs down the stairs and then outside, slamming the door. Another pane of glass falls to the floor. Wendy continues to cry, and then she won't let me hug her. She runs downstairs and out of the house.

I experience a hollow satisfaction in finally getting my way. I am king of the house, my house, me alone.

WHEN I AM LIVING among my species, I feel a lot like the character in the Woody Allen movie *Deconstructing Harry*. Robin Williams plays an actor who, during a film shoot, begins to appear "a little soft." The cameraman is unable to get him in focus, and the director calls it a day, telling the distressed actor, "Go home, get it together, you know, *focus*." As time goes on the affliction gets worse. His wife explains to the children that "Daddy isn't feeling very well," and eventually the whole family puts on thick glasses that keep Daddy in focus. The glasses also happen to make the rest of the world appear blurry, the price paid for a preferred clarity.

. . . And so I wonder about isolation and what that will do to me and my family. How much socialization is required to keep one *in focus*?

• • •

DAY 94

Grumpy morning with yesterday's scene floating about like the smell of rotting squid. Thanks to Stephan's ability to apologize, and Wendy's to smooth things over, all of our moods are okay by the afternoon. It seems I just do the asshole part, and they do the rest.

Sometimes I thought my dad was a jerk. Now I'm the jerk. I thought I'd be different, a different kind of dad with only the good qualities of my own choosing. That's the kind of parent I expected myself to be: a *generation improved*. Instead I've stepped off a cliff and feel like I am having a stupid argument with gravity. I remember all that my dad put up with from me, and I am so many miles away from having that kind of capacity to endure Stephan.

It is getting colder now. The days can be brilliantly crisp, the view from our windows unlimited. We collect all the tree branches and cuttings from around where we built the dock and make a big fire on the beach at low tide. I chain-saw a small woodpile for the fishing shack, which burns wood too hot and fast in the small stove. Still, it's somewhere I can escape to.

DAY 95

A big herd of great blue herons flew over the house as the sun rose this morning. Wendy almost fell off the bed looking after them. Bear watches Wendy make breakfast and his big wet drools spill out onto his fur, and then the floor.

Today there are eleven tuna-fishing boats within sight. They fish with their lines connected to kites and then connected to live bait. Peter explains that the kites' erratic movements entice the big fish. A few years ago one of these boats caught a thirteen-hundred-pound tuna, which, because of its quality and the market price at that moment, sold for $33,000. By noon I count thirty-eight boats.

DAY 98

Stephan

Daniel set up a target for me hanging from the trees and I shot it all day. It's awesome.

7. Boys

> We cannot but pity the boy who has never fired a gun;
> he is no more humane, while his education has been
> sadly neglected.
>
> — THOREAU

DAY 105
It is wonderful to see the *Lise and Kathleen* come bounding around the south side of the island, around three in the afternoon. Mike and Aaron show up with beer. Mike is Peter's older brother, tough, like rawhide. He is definitely not someone you'd want to be stranded with on a deserted island. He'd be real stringy eating.

Mike also brings some dead ducks, the currency of a good neighbor.

After a bit all the guys pile into the *Lise and Kathleen* for a ride to Mike's nearby camp. A camp refers to a hut or shed that is 1) hard to get to, 2) where you store your lobster traps, nets, bait, and so on, 3) where your wife almost never visits—and can't without you bringing her anyway, and 4) where you and nobody else set the standard for exactly what constitutes a clean dish.

On the way Aaron falls overboard. He had been quiet until then, but suddenly becomes wonderfully animated. *"Holy shit, goddamn! I'm fuckin' dying here, give me a hand up, would ya?"* I've always enjoyed how sudden and unexpected immersion brings a wonderful dose of screaming authenticity to a person.

At the camp Mike brings out the gun and shoots with Stephan. The woodstove crackles as some duck stew boils away. Stephan drives our boat home with me mumbling suggestions from the bow.

ALL OF THE MEN here are bound to one another through the ocean. I know we could not talk about this directly; it is too poetic and close to who we are for words. The ocean is what flows through our veins. It is that deeply in us, so unconscious and powerful. The beer and the guns are merely safe ways for us to share it with one another, get our feet wet, a convenient distraction from that which we cannot speak of. I am glad that Stephan is being exposed to this.

DAY 106

Sometimes I get bleary of paying attention to now, of matters that are "important," like *are Wendy and I having a fight?* I reach over and put a hand on her sleeping shoulder. With groggy animation my hand is removed. So I guess we are fighting about something.

The strange thing for me is a feeling that it probably really was me who did something—whatever it is we are fighting about. It's not so much that I am wrong, or did a bad thing; it's more likely I just did not notice what was falling out of my mouth. There is a very short cable between my mind and my mouth. When she asks me something like "Do I look fat in these pants?" I assume it's really a question, and that I should answer truthfully. (Wrong!)

Stephan made us pizza for dinner. He's enjoying reading this year's ten most banned books, which a friend in Idaho sent him. (I can't think of a better way to get a kid to read.)

DAY 107

Great afternoon walk around the island, Stephan wearing his long underwear and greatly resembling a young and depressed Santa Claus being told he did not get a part in the Christmas pageant. He's beginning to do that teenage thing of trying to look miserable.

Wendy and I argue for a minute and to end it I just look away and go back to the book I'm reading. I hear "But Daniel" and look up to see her face undergo the transition from sadness to tears—the whole process—in maybe five seconds. And then she looks away, having had the ultimate end of any argument, the last word of Tears.

I offer Wendy a sense of safety. I am her knight in armor, the protector. The conflict is that in my eyes I can do this only in my world, on this island. Here I can build shelter, create warmth and comfort, prepare for emergencies, supply power and water, and ensure safety from most worldly demons. That's why I'm here! And so elated to have a well-defined purpose in my life. But Wendy, she wants to meet people, to work, drink lattes, go to yard sales, eat frozen yogurt. So how is it our lives are woven together, our wants, needs, and dreams entwined, our souls wonderfully tangled?

DAY 108
Gloomy rainy day.

DAY 110
Burnt fried spaghetti for breakfast. Stephan and I do schoolwork while Wendy repaints the porch door and chairs. We've begun using the woodstove, a real sweet friend to visit day and night, luscious heat.

Rainy storm. Several new leaks develop where the rain is being driven up and under the roof shingles. I'm trying to convince myself that *any* asshole can build a house that *doesn't* leak.

Wendy
Daniel is home-schooling Stephan, which is a very brave thing. I would be unable to do this part. I love the quiet time this brings for me. Daniel has Stephan do his work either at the desk in the small hut or outside if it's nice weather. Daniel is very patient with Stephan, giving him lots of extra information and making sure he's looking at things from several different viewpoints. The curriculum we chose is Christian-based because it was the

most challenging and advanced. But since Daniel is Jewish, he comes with a totally different take on things. He challenges Stephan to look at what he's being taught and what his heart tells him to be the truth for him. In the hut there are war marks on the wall where Stephan sits to do his work—big black scuff marks from his boots.

DAY 113

Stephan and I drive for hours to a town called Hill River, where, I'm told, a lady sells rabbits. I assumed they would be big, wild, and vicious beasts ready to breed and survive on an island, laugh at blizzards, and frighten small children. In a few years we could hunt them and always have food. Turns out they are the old petting-zoo rabbits —as in too old to survive the rigors of getting petted. "But we drove all this way, and don't they look kinda cute with those big floppy ears?" Stephan says. So in the back of the truck they go, six of the cuddliest rabbits you'd never want to eat. One is dead by the time we stop at the town's only red light.

Three hours later we release the remaining five on the island. They look at us sadly, motionless. Bear and Abby are barely held by Stephan. I run at the plump little fellows, waving and screaming, hoping they'll scatter. One nibbles some grass.

Stephan

We went into town today to go to a flea market, and I got to eat onion rings.

Then we got rabbits, and the dog's already killed one.

I buried it and gave it a big gravestone. Now I am reading *Watership Down*.

DAY 116
West-southwest gale. Bear proudly shows off a black bunny he has obviously been chewing on since dawn. Four to go. Stephan had to clean his room and he found some dishes we've been missing.

DAY 117
Quote of the morning from the radio: "Investors ignored the early-warning signs of fraud, when the gold mine's geologist committed suicide . . ."

Stephan has been singing from my *Rocky Horror* CD all day. What do you say to your eleven-year-old when he's yelling, "I'm just a sweet transvestite . . . from transsexual . . . Transylvania . . . ah ah"?

Naturally I am disgusted, but the fact that it's my CD and I have every song fully memorized prevents me from saying anything. I hum along.

DAY 124—NOVEMBER
We wake to a cold and brilliant blue morning. Wendy overenthusiastically flushes the toilet and one of the small plastic pieces of the "flush mechanism" explodes with a twang, vanishing forever (I guess it's with all the unmatched socks).

Gorgeous day. Peter and Mike stop by for a yarn as I'm fixing a leak in the motorboat.

When we met years ago interactions were tense—me

the rich, overeducated, New York, Green Peacing privileged snotty blah blah blah. Now I'm called over to have a beer. I've hunted with them, and we've shared a hangover or two. A man is finally a man in his own eyes when he knows himself among other men, when he's on a team, one of the guys.

DAY 125

Stephan is banned from the house for the day because he threw a tremendous fit, complete with tears, yelling, and door slamming. This one had to do with a Monopoly game that he was close to losing. Did my parents let me win games? Is that what I am supposed to do? Again the zucchini thing. Am I forever doomed to be so selfish with Stephan? Am I the dad or another child?

We find the remains of another rabbit, so that's three down. When next Bear comes by I tell him to stop pretending he isn't a corpse-chewing murderer. Then Aaron and a friend of his show up and, only to be polite, of course, I offer them a drink, and, well, one thing leads to another.

Getting drunk with Aaron is a privilege. He's about five foot six and two hundred pounds of muscle. The thing I like about him is his smile, his open look right back at you that is simply friendly. Aaron is someone who you want to stand by you in a bar fight or a gale. He is loyal.

As they leave, Aaron throws Stephan and me two ducks from the bottom of his boat. I want to nurse one of them back to health because it isn't quite dead. But it's dinnertime, and I think it is important to know exactly how food shows up on your plate. I break its neck. Then when I cut its head off the duck runs around in circles to Stephan's (and my own) shrieks. Luckily our manhood is not questioned, as Aaron's boat is already weaving out of the harbor.

8. Our World

Cease to be ruled by dogmas and authorities;
look at the world!

—ROGER BACON

DAY 126

Wendy

Daniel and I had a very small wedding, about fifty people. We had sushi and shish kebab catered. Daniel made all of our invitations by hand. He took old sea charts and cut them up. He wrote everything by hand on every invitation. Then he got a roll of wax paper, you know like for your kitchen, and cut a piece for inside each invite and then sealed them with a piece of duct tape. People loved them—it was so Daniel. We were married by a woman who is a wonderfully enlightened minister. At the beginning of the ceremony she had us give our mothers each a rose to acknowledge them. When the ceremony was over Daniel's best friend put on ABBA's "Take a Chance on Me."

During Stephan's history class today some creative re-wording of his book's text was unavoidable. The Christian-based home-schooling books we have are excellent, but I am, after all, a liberal New York Jewish guy, so we modified "In 1492 Christopher Columbus discovered America" to "In 1492 America was invaded by . . ." Later, "The missionaries were the only true friends of the Indians" became "Although responsible for the destruc-tion of the entire Native American culture, the mission-aries generally smiled when at work." In the geology section, where it says, "Some scientists actually consider the possibility that the continents drift and at one time were . . ." we changed it to "About 1 percent of the espe-cially inept geology graduate students continue to wrestle with the theory of plate tectonics." I'm particularly proud of that one.

Stephan
I hate Daniel, he made me clean up my room.

DAY 127
Stephan
I love Daniel, he took me for a boat ride today.

DAY 128
"Daniel, did the fridge flood again?"

"I'm ignoring the fridge, dear."

During the day the upstairs is usually quite warm, es-pecially since the stove is burning. The idea with the fridge was to have a cool box, not for ice cream or anything that really needs to be cold, but for eggs, cheese, cabbage. Even milk will last a day or three in there. Just leaving things outside in the shade doesn't work, because what the dogs don't eat freezes at night. But, the earth that the fridge is buried in will stay at a pretty constant temperature. A good plan, it's just that most anything that spills upstairs ends up downstairs. That is because the second floor's floorboards have dried and shrunk so much that the upstairs works like a giant colander, but that is quite another issue. The end result is that whenever you get down on your knees, pull open the trap door, and reach in, you never know just what you will find. That's why you will often hear Wendy or me asking Stephan to bring up this or that from the fridge.

Actually there are two bins side by side under the trap door. On the right we keep all the stuff not easily bruised, like beer, jelly, a layer of regular and sweet potatoes, onions, cabbages, and carrots. As this neatly stacked arrangement works only if you come at it from the top down (*"Hey, let's have some carrots and cabbage for a snack, potatoes for dinner, then a lot of jelly and beer for dessert!"*), entropy has its way, and it is usually a frightful mess in there. Many a meal begins with "Hey, Stephan, grab five things from the right bin."

The left bin is more dangerous; it's all soft. Right after a shore visit it may contain butter, eggs, cheese, a thawing surprise like hamburger, or even frozen pizza. The left bin also contains the *leftovers*.

My mother always told me to only eat what I liked, and not to stuff myself. As a result of this attempt to raise me properly, I have rebelled. I will eat anything, including a worm when I was properly dared by a pretty girl. I still not only finish all of my food but will then eat from other people's plates until the table is cleared. But if there has been a major miscalculation in the amount of food made—that is, if I've gone through all the heroic efforts of "saving" an awful meal with curry and chili and ketchup and, finally, red pepper, and Wendy has politely said that she's not hungry—well then, we do have *leftovers*.

I don't know if Wendy and Stephan have an actual conspiracy against me or if things from the left bin are actually escaping. My point is that few of my leftovers have ever returned from the fridge. I send them down, plan on how I might resurrect them the next day in a "Lazarus stew," and then they vanish. Perhaps they have decomposed into a splendid sediment slushy that will one day baffle a geology graduate student. All I know is that I will never reach into the left bin and the dogs are getting fat.

DAY 129

Wendy confesses to finding another dead rabbit, so now we're down to two.

Abby vomited during dinner, a rabbit foot. This only briefly interrupted her begging us for spaghetti, of which she got none, so she re-ate the foot.

I became so sad today reading a letter from some

friends in Idaho: "The pictures you sent us are wonderful and your life seems so much like what we dream about, but the bills keep us locked here." People hang on to their excuses as if they were a commodity in short supply.

DAY 133

Another dead rabbit in the morning. I hear him scream, a humanlike sound that is truly frightening. Hearing it dumps adrenaline into my system. When I get him out of Bear's mouth his back is broken, so I kill and bury him—no heart to turn him into stew, as was originally planned.

We walk around the island and stop at our bog. It's about as big as a football field and so soft you can jump up and land headfirst laughing. We are rolling in the thick moss when I show Stephan a primitive living skill I learned years ago. By holding and squeezing a wet clump of moss over your mouth you can drink. The cool part is how you aim your thumb at your thirst (that is, you hold your fist up so the water from the wet moss runs down your thumb and into your mouth). First Stephan squeezes the moss before holding it up and gets his lap wet. Then on his second try he aims too low and gets his belly wet. Clearly a being who can operate a TV remote and cannot get a drink of water if his life depended on it couldn't have *evolved* from anything. So much for my theory of evolution.

Two weeks ago in Galeville there were paper turkeys in every store window for Thanksgiving. Why would I think about the harvest, a time of thanks for living, anything like that? What organic input did my former life contain where I could be in touch with a natural cycle? I relied on specials on stuffing to alert me to a seasonal change. Thanksgiving. Thank spending, Thanks pending.

I hate going ashore now. On the island I have a place. Ashore I am entangled in a web of triviality, and I just want to sit down and cry for the vagueness of my life. Wendy flourishes like a spider in the center of its web, rejoicing in the vibrations of each silken string.

Today, ashore for laundry and shopping, we stop for a hitchhiker. The first thing you notice about Albert when you pick him up for his weekly trip into town is that his clothes don't fit right. My first thought about him was that he wasn't operating on all thrusters. Listening to him took some focus; the words were chopped, accented. He's such a wild character, like he's out of a novel, that you can barely talk with him in real life.

Albert rows a small red dory along the coast and combs beaches, primarily in search of firewood. If it's not storming, he's on the water. I have seen him before, I just never really noticed him. A lone boat working along the coast—as common as a herring gull, and not as noisy. He has always lived alone. He grew up across Kingsland's harbor in Young Cove some fifty years ago. Junior's wife, Becky, also grew up there. Ten or so families lived in this tiny community, which no road led to. They would row the mile to Kingsland, or walk if the ice was thick. Today Young Cove is a favorite safe and secluded anchorage for visiting yachts. Ashore you can find some graves and a foundation or two.

Albert will row his dory as far as Whale Island, a good three-hour row. He gathers firewood for his cooking and heating stove. There is a huge brush pile by his house, a small shack you assume is abandoned. The woodpile is twice the size of the shack, which resembles something a Stephen King character would pause at before entering.

Albert is immune to social graces. He is the person in Kingsland whom everyone cares for, a test of their conscience, perhaps. Whenever you have given him a lift into town you find a religious pamphlet suggesting you accept Jesus, and accept him soon. You never actually see him leave it on the car seat, or maybe the floor. I think he wants you to find it as if its appearance was a small miracle. The first time I found one I was deeply struck with love for him. A man wanting to share his God is inspiring to me, the rawness of it. A man wanting to impose his God—that's ugly. But the two should not be confused.

DAY 134

Stephan swims daily and ecstatically. His joy is the best thing to remind me that he's just a kid. It's okay if his room looks like a bomb went off, or if he chews with his mouth so open that if you took a picture, you wouldn't necessarily know which way the food was going. These are the fun things for him. I need to step back and let him have joy instead of corrections. If I could just do that.

The dogs killed the last rabbit this afternoon. That ends the sustainable-food-supply idea. Martini hour was

moved up to three o'clock, after which I thought of building a still to replace the rabbits.

DAY 137

The seat for our outhouse is a sperm-whale vertebrae—
one of the biggest ones, the first or second from the skull.
What is so special about this "seat" is how perfectly the
human ass fits into it. When you sit you are so comfortable that you barely know you're sitting. It's like when
you were learning not to pee in bed and you had dreams
that justified your accidents. like "I'm getting up . . .
going to the bathroom" or "Well, I'm in the *bathtub,* so
it's okay . . ." or whatever, but it was so comfortable and
warm for a while, to sleep in your pee, it just felt good,
peaceful. Unfortunately, we had to learn that this feeling
of well-being was bad; an angry mother changing the
sheets may love you, but enough is enough. So now when
you sit in this outhouse it feels so good that you not only
can't pee, you have an urge to go into therapy.

DAY 147

I am proud that we have our own dump out here, our
own pile of refuse. We do not carry our garbage ashore to
vanish somewhere else. And not just that, but with my
master's degree in environmental science, only I can take
the blame for locating this dump on a hilltop just thirty
feet from our one small well! So you see, my island, my
brave new world, has all the comforts of civilization and
no one to blame, no *they,* only *I.* We bust glass on a rock

just where the waves reach, recycling that back into sand. Soda cans we carry ashore for recycling, and everything else we burn, either for heat or in our fifty-five-gallon burn barrel. I think all of the world's environmental problems would be solved if getting rid of your waste was your own problem, and you could not pay someone else to handle it for you.

9. Winter

> I have always been regretting that I was not as wise
> as the day I was born. The intellect is a cleaver; it
> discerns and rifts its way into the secret of things.
>
> —THOREAU

DAY 148

Beautiful shooting stars all night, followed by full-on meteor storm near dawn. Wendy was afraid there wouldn't be enough stars around for tomorrow night. We could see smoke trails in the dawning sky. Sharing a shooting star with someone you are in love with is a perfect moment. We also watched a UFO, which looked like a shot flare under a parachute. Stephan decided it was a scout ship from Zafron 3, a small world in the Delta quadrant.

The weather's closing in now. Less sunlight on the clear days, and three out of seven days we are unable to leave the island. The seas form a wonderful barrier of surf at the harbor mouth.

I am a wilderness emergency medical technician and have a small hospital of supplies in a big backpack. We are prepared for anything up to the sort of injury where you look into some brand-new body cavity. Weather permitting, we can get to a hospital in two hours.

We have everything from splints to Chap Stick, sutures to baby powder. In my experience, the body takes pretty good care of itself, so no worries, and a little prayer maybe.

With the reduced sunlight we're sleeping like hibernating bears, getting some chubbiness as winter sets in. Daylight hours are only slightly less than in Idaho, but here we are living practically outdoors. Yes, we are dry and warm, but our home is mostly glass. Our internal clocks are in sync with nature, not the ten o'clock news. When the sun sets we become sleepy. We rise at dawn, and the sunrise signals our breakfast.

Every month we cross to the mainland to get a big package of all our mail from Idaho. Last week Wendy got a skiing exercise machine and she's trying to get me on it. My pathetic response is "Are you kidding? I'm a second-degree black belt! I used to do push-ups on my fingertips! I could kick Captain Kirk's ass!"

The machine is set up downstairs . . . a four-hundred-dollar exercise machine on an island seven miles from— I can't even say it. But it is funny to hear her skiing away. She wears her headphones, so every day the house trembles and these maniacal off-key shrieks are yelled out. Since Wendy has been listening to my generation's music only since we've been married, her brain is not filled with the lyrics from every Rolling Stone album. Today the house shudders to "I can't get no sanitation."

I guess during an exercise frenzy the words don't have to fit with the song, but none of it seems to fit with the island. I should throw Wendy's health magazines over the side when I boat the mail from shore.

DAY 150—DECEMBER

The first snow is on the ground and the dogs are barking at it with enthusiasm. Unlike dogs, we are blessed with the ability to define and separate, to label. Or maybe it's a sort of a curse. These labels are also what make us lonely.

I love a snowstorm because it unites all things by texture. From a patch of wild asparagus to a bulldozer, it's all white, soft, cold, and tastes the same. Definitions don't work; everything is just *one thing*. What else unites us so? When I am having an episode of manic enlightenment I see peoples soul's this way, exactly equal as if we were all caught in a snowstorm together.

DAY 151

Today the wind was blowing twenty-five knots, and the seas as big as I'd like to run into with this small aluminum boat. Foam and spray, even some green water over the bow (that is a phrase sailors use to describe a lot of water where there should only be heavy spray, at worst). I surfed down the big waves. I like to go alone because Wendy and Stephan get really scared. As I return I'm drenched. Icicles hang from my sleeves. I make a lunge for the boat ramp and then fall into the shallow water as the dogs engulf me in eager greetings. I secure the boat, stagger up the trail, slip down the one small hill, crawl into the house, and collapse, holding out the package. It's warm inside. Wendy has just baked a loaf of rye bread.

Still wet, I tear into the mail and am reminded of a strange world I once lived in. I sort the bills, which means I give them to Wendy. The last time I balanced the checkbook I was $2,000 off. I get a cool army-surplus catalog, and I absolutely must have the "recently discovered in an old warehouse authentic WWI German motorcycle messenger goggle's case."

There is a heap of junk mail, total trash. It is hard to be a victim out here, and I've become proactive in my asking to be taken off mailing lists. To the NRA I write: "I'm a liberal pro-gun-control fanatic. I have fantasies of Sarah Brady. Please take my name off your mailing list." Idaho public television gets "I hate TV, I moved to the only place I could find without reception. Please take my name off your mailing list." To the company advertising "STAY HARD for INTIMACY," I write: "My dick is hard, thank you. I have lots of sex, I'm fine! Leave me alone!" My old grade school gets "Look, I really did not like this school and that is why I left in the fifth grade, so please . . ." And finally, to a company offering a cologne "GUARANTEED to get you all the pretty women you want, no matter what you look like . . . without even *trying*," I write, "Due to a serious accident, my penis has been removed. Desist these mailings or I will sue your ass for the emotional trauma they are causing." I wonder how I got on that mailing list—either from those "virile" pills I got two years ago or from the "burn fat while you sleep" pills (hence the "no matter what you look like"). I wonder why I've gotten no hair-loss ads this month.

I so appreciate the perspective gained by distancing myself from our culture. I'm just not smart enough to be alert when I'm swimming in it. Here is an ad for a "golden bookmark from rain-forest leaves." Somebody is actually promoting a product made of cut rain-forest leaves to promote saving . . . oh hell, it's just too ridiculous. The ad covers its own ugly ass immediately with "handpicked by rain-forest natives." They douse each leaf in copper then eighteen-karat gold, and you can own it. This is such a pure absurdity that I think it should have its own place on the periodic table. The rest of my junk mail I just stamp with my DECEASED—RETURN TO SENDER stamp.

DAY 154

I've decided to go hunt with Peter. I don't know if I'll really pull the trigger on Bambi, but it's been years since I allowed myself to crawl in muck and slither inside an aware animal's radar. I want that excitement. In Maine I almost touched a deer. I'd camouflaged myself—mostly by being pretty naked and rolling in a fire pit. Then oh so slowly, using the hairs on my skin to feel with, I crept to a deer trail I'd found the night before. I dozed off, but then woke up with a doe about four feet away. That, to me, is hunting.

Somehow I have Peter convinced that I am a great wilderness man. We meet before sunrise at his father's wharf and are off in one of his wooden boats. We motor into a small cove, the same one Peter's mother lived in when she was a kid.

We snake up a tributary for miles, finally running out of deep water. We tie the boat up to a tree and continue on foot over some rocky shallows until we find the small rowboat Peter leaves where the water gets deep enough again to continue. We row over a pond of thin ice, leaving beautiful patterns where our paddles break through.

"Hunting"? The word is overused, certainly misused anyway. I would call what I did "lost with a gun." Peter was fine—happy to be alive and with purpose even. I fell into a stream (after breaking through the ice and bashing my shins), sat on a mutated giant thorn, and during the ten minutes I was separated from Peter experienced fear and hunger like that of the Donner party.

Hours later we stumbled into Peter's camp to celebrate nothing more than the glory of being alive at sunrise. (That may sound good, but actually I was half frozen and unwilling to let Peter know.) Beans, meat, beer, and white bread. Boy, am I old. One beer before noon and I'm a-grog all the rest of the day.

Wendy housewived and was happy to see me when I returned. She'd eaten a whole can of Pringles. Now she's making cookies and drinking a martini. I lie in the sun and Wendy brings me assorted crackers and cheese. It is great when I can convince her I just did something heroic for her: "I thought of your starving face so I pulled my-self out of the water and crawled on. My clothes were a sheet of ice. I had to carry Peter to safety, and the snakes . . ." She cares for me for as long as I can nurse it—four hours so far, and in a minute I'll bring up frostbite and how I don't *think* its too bad ("but I didn't want to worry you"). That'll bring me to about lunch tomorrow. ("Oh just some soup, dear . . . and a tuna sandwich. . . . Can you hard-boil me some eggs? . . . No, I want the crusts cut off . . . triangles please. . . . could you hand me that pillow?")

DAY 157

Just Wendy and I walked around the island today. The sun was warm and we lay on our bellies at Pebble Beach and dug ourselves in, scooping warmed pebbles onto our backs. We collected Christmas presents, only the most beautiful stones, each one telling its own geological story. Certainly the least stressful Christmas shopping ever. The dogs went dipping in and out, Abby eating sea urchins and anything else dead. You would think eating sea urchins would be difficult, like trying to swallow a por-cupine ass first. But Abby shows relentless commitment to whatever she is doing, blessed with the sort of igno-rance that leads to discovery.

OH MY GOSH!

The best meals I prepare are usually in the *Oh my gosh!* category. It is called that for the simple reason that four out of five meals served in this style begin or end with one or more of the diners exclaiming, *"Oh my gosh!"*

OMG meal preparation takes more self-confidence than most people have. Four out of five failures is enough for an average person to recognize as feedback. But not me; I take it as a challenge.

The rules for OMG cooking are simple. All OMG meals must be cooked in one pot. They must consist of 20 to 80 percent leftovers. It should be colorful. An onion must be present.

Since we have the name OMG at our disposal already, you not need bother boxing yourself in with any other name. Soufflé, stew, stir-fry, roast . . . these limit your creativity. Make something the likes of which has never before appeared on any table!

What usually happens is that the initial thematic flavor scheme crumbles. For this reason the food must be taste-tested often. Beginning with a subtle flavor like dill or basil is fine. Just don't count on it. And never, ever answer with specifics when someone asks, "What's for dinner?"

To really be an OMG chef you must think of yourself as a hero, someone who enjoys risk.

As soon as you are willing to admit the failure of the basil theme, the fun begins. First use soy sauce or tamari. Next pepper, lots of pepper. Then sugar. Now it is important to taste the food. If it's edible, yell, "Food!" quickly, before an impulse will cause you to add something offensive. If it is not yet edible (most likely it *was* edible ten minutes earlier and you missed it), you must attempt a massive food-group reorientation. Gloves are good from here on out. Try tomato sauce. If no good, go on to ketchup. If you still can't eat it, go on to curry. Be careful here, because all you have left is a single magic bullet, and that is chili powder.

Thus the dogs and I eat well. Wendy and Stephan eat a lot of crackers.

DAY 158

Dogs couldn't have pockets. They live too much in the here and now. Human deviation from nature came with the first pocket. Adam and Eve were thrown out of Eden and thus began wearing clothes with pockets. A dog is so much in the moment because it has nowhere to put anything that is not in its mouth. Which came first, the pocket or the desire to have a pocket? Ever seen a dog wearing one of those doggie backpacks? They look miserable, absolutely miserable.

I envy having no concept of keeping. I watch Abby find a big stinky dead lobster on the shore and see her agony looking at us, it, us, it . . . as she realizes that she cannot both come with us and eat it. She must decide, us or it. She whines in confusion, but finally chooses us and looks back only once.

Another meteor shower and we all lie on the rocks wrapped in blankets. The stars rain toward us in lightning streaks. No matter how many flash by we cry out in *ooh*s and *aah*s, unable to remain silent. Miracles do not become humdrum. We share brilliant shooting-star moments.

DAY 162

I drink coffee bitter black to remind me that it is a wonderful luxury not to be made mediocre by repetition. As a wilderness guide in the Idaho desert, I was hungry and ate mice, rats, snakes, deer, porcupines, and marmots. Nothing tastes so good as cooked meat when you are really hungry, when your body is craving protein, when a voice hidden way under a lot of cultural evolution still yells *Eat meat now!* How excellent to fall into my body's physical hardware. I'm so sick of the psychological hard drive. When the body rules, when that primal voice speaks, I can't help but listen. It's like having God talk to me—inarguable, completely in harmony and perfect.

I hope everyone gets to feel it, the righteous burning that God wants them to do this or that and that they are just a vessel, a means through and for which living happens, that all their petty shit and even major neuroses can be put aside for something bigger. It's like a full-moon spring tide—it's a force, a feeling well worth dying for.

DAY 163

It is so windy right now that a strange bird I've never seen before is hiding in the harbor. Just twenty feet out from his shelter—a big rock outcropping—whitecaps are flying by. He's black and white, a seabird, and his bill is sort of thick, hooked, and black, and his head is pointy like a merganser's. How ridiculous to find a name so I don't have to look at the creature before me anymore! I have him pegged, page 79 in the bird book.

In the afternoon we write our "Christmas letter," which helps us sort out our friends into two categories. First are those who will laugh, and then those who will become concerned.

Dear———,

We were gonna write one of those happy finger-down-your-throat letters about the joys of blah blah blah. The truth is: 1) This letter was mass produced; 2) We're probably only sending it to you 'cause you wrote us first and we feel bad; or 3) We hope you forgot to send us one so now you'll feel bad.

Well, the New Hays Family has had a crappy year. We lost money on the sale of our Idaho house and Stephan has begun saying "No." (He's eleven. Feel free to send advice, survival tips.) Wendy continues to "prime" sexually, while I ease into my decline. I got Viagra and that helps some, but I have also upped my Prozac dose to handle the stress. Stephan has begun getting zits. Wendy and I are gaining weight. I'm still losing my hair.

As far as Christmas gifts go, please send us self-addressed envelopes and we'll send you a bill (hurry for January Visa statements). That's what we want, for you to share in our seasonal happiness by paying our bills.

Our joyful motto for the New Year is "Things would only be a little worse if we was laying down in a hearse." Secretly, we hope we're doing better than you.

With mixed feelings,

Dan, Wendy, and Stephan

DAY 165

Windy night. Walk around the island, grilled-cheese sandwiches for breakfast. Wonderful shortwave radio listening, where I suppose the irony of hearing about the United
States bombing Baghdad followed by a commercial about
bad breath is lost. They get equal air time, thirty seconds.

I found the body of the bird I watched yesterday, I
could tell it was sick. I looked at it for almost an hour. I
certainly could not have designed anything so exquisite,
so perfect. It embarrasses me when I compare it to my
own creations.

DAY 166

Today is electrical-crisis day. The wind's been north to
northwest for eight days now, and the windmill is in its
comfy wind hollow behind a hill. (Any jerk can put a
windmill where there is wind.) The batteries were down
to 8.6 volts this morning, so now we've rigged up the
three solar panels and can use the laptop. I'm trying to
print a résumé, but the converter alarm keeps hinting at
insufficient electrical funds and the printer dies midletter
whenever a cloud floats by. I have always encountered
such exceptional obstacles when attempting to produce a
résumé that I no longer even question my unconscious
motives.

In college I loved going to the table of ten new computers in the library and one by one asking them to count
all the books they had access to. They were "fast" then,
but now a calculator does more. By the time I got the

tenth going the lights would dim and everything would be slowed back to human speed. Even the blinking cursors were slower, and I would know I'd done good in the world that day.

Another electrical event of great importance was tonight's unveiling of the Christmas lights. Leave it to a rural Nova Scotian hardware store to have battery-operated Christmas lights. Two C batteries—rechargeable by windmill—will last four hours. We hang them up and it really does trigger a Christmas spirit, like a flow of endorphins. Since it is dark at four-thirty, any lights help.

DAY 167

Late at night I often fiddle with a shortwave radio receiver I've had since I was a kid. It is best if the sky is perfectly clear and the wind is from the north (less moisture). I listen to music from India, or maybe the news from countries other than the United States or Canada. It is good to hear that things seem to happen outside of this continent. I find my culture to be a tad self-centered.

I have even been able to get a station in New York City! Thank God for Dr. Laura. She is the only high-intensity Jewish girl heard in this house. I got on the show once and her thoughts were valid, although too direct for me to hear. A hazard of a two-minute therapy session, I guess. Anyway, for no reason I can conjure, Wendy hates her and yells, "Shut up!" at my little radio. Many colorful and energetic discussions begin this way. Wendy says Dr. Laura is rude and insensitive. I reply, "Yeah, it's refreshing, isn't it?" Then Wendy says she doesn't let people tell their whole story and I say, "Yah, like the story matters," and so on. After all the counseling I've done with teens (for the past ten years) and the careful rapport building I do to let them hear truths gently, I just love how this woman spills it out. Perhaps her radio therapy is not so helpful for the twenty people she handles a day, but to the people who listen, it's clear, insightful, and, once spoken, often becomes the henceforth obvious.

I loved living in Idaho because, among other things, it taught me about guns, and owning my first gun taught me something about life: every moment I don't shoot myself in the head, I am reminded that living is my choice. Radio DJs' phrases like "hump day" or "thank God it's Friday" really piss me off. VICTIMS!! By not shooting myself I have consciously chosen to be alive, and so having guns reminds me to *shut up and get with the program*. That simple sentence is the point of all therapy. Somehow a bullet can miraculously condense years of counseling into a single sentence, what therapists and psychiatrists don't want you to know. The short course. It works for me because to stay undead makes me a *verb* choosing to live. *That* I got owning my first gun. Not bad.

DAY 168

Wendy and I have taken to lots of loud yelling and cussing and I recommend this therapeutically for stress release. She yells, "You do it now, damnit!" (Meaning hand-write twelve copies of our full-page Christmas letter.) I yell back, "We can wait to go ashore to a Xerox machine." She says, "Okay, just only five, please. Please?" Later we compromise, and I write all twelve letters.

DAY 169

Howling east-wind storming day. I run between the electrical and water systems like an eager dad—chlorinating here, plugging in the saw charger there, siphoning off twenty gallons into extra tanks, disconnecting an old 12-volt battery that finally holds a charge ("Honey, I *saved* this battery—call your mom, I'm a Baptist now!"), and so on. I just love our systems, the independence, the contact with our environment.

It's a power-coffee day. When I played ice-hockey goalie in tenth grade I used to use caffeine as my secret weapon, my one and only strategy, since skill was not an option. Half a cup of instant coffee crystals, a quarter cup of sugar, a quarter cup of water. I'd drink this sludge thirty minutes before game time and went from being a fair goalie to an okay goalie. The problem was, I couldn't skate either way, but with this jitter-mix cocktail in me I just vibrated around and was thus in more than one place at any given moment, sort of like an electron. Often when a puck came by it would hit me, and if I happened to fall forward I would land on it and my teammates would come by and hit my pads with their sticks and say "Good save" and I felt good. I remember once boldly skating twenty feet from the net. Someone on the other team broke free and rushed at me. I was just able to keep my balance as I skated backward. I remember being surprised when I passed the goal net, but then I knocked myself out hitting the backboards. I figure if you really suck at a sport, get a concussion early in the season so you have something to not quite have recovered from for the rest of the season.

So it's a coffee day. I play with our laptop. Since we had it fixed before we came here I haven't been able to confuse it into busting again. I start pulling out its battery and disconnecting the power cord at the same time and am satisfied to see a sort of freezing sleet form over the "Welcome to Macintosh" smile face. It blinks twice and makes some boinging noises, then shuts off. Wendy is pissed at me—she's the typist—but I feel good; another triumph for Dankind over the evil-machine empire. (It's the sort of day where I must struggle to find meaning.)

One hundred pages into *The Fountainhead* Wendy announces, "My heart is broken, I'm done with the book." I point out that there are 350 pages left, and she should keep going.

Last month Stephan got to the part in *The Princess Bride* where the hero dies. He burst into tears and threw the book into the ocean. I waded in, dried it off, and read it to him until the hero came back to life. He snuffled a little, and then he took the book back.

Somehow this was an important fatherly moment for me. Something made Stephan unhappy, and I knew how to fix it. I could make him happy again, and I didn't even need to be *right* about anything. I want desperately to have an unconscious ability to father well, a prehistoric ability to love at all times. Thinking about what to do seems so pathetic. But this one thing I did right.

DAY 170

Wendy is baking fiendishly. For New Year's we're giving a cake to Junior and Becky, a loaf of bread to Peter and Mary Ellen, brownies to Mike, and so on. She's upset because she can't cut pieces out of the final things; they have to be given whole. I watch as she eats spoonfuls of batter, trying to fill up her cravings before the actual baking begins. Even the dogs stare in wonder, because usually they get to lick a spoon or a bowl, but not today. I'm hungry but she won't give me anything. I go downstairs and snack on Bear and Abby's dried food, which actually is pretty good.

One of Wendy's creations is what she calls "Special K bars." I grew up in Manhattan eating exotic eastern European cakes from Collette's, baklava, and Russian Tea Room pastries, imported directly from only the most exotic of countries. "Special K bars" are made from sugar, Karo syrup, peanut butter, sugar, chocolate chips, Special K cereal, and some more sugar. I am wondering if my own evolutionary ladder travels up, down, or sideways.

The house shakes. I luxuriate in remembering drilling into bedrock the sixteen holes that secure us to the rocks. I know what holds us to the earth here, and that warms me. I know how the nails connect the wood to frames to roofs to walls . . . and I know where to stand to avoid accidentally noticing where I can see outside other than through a window or door.

When I go ashore for the mail I meet Becky by our shared mailbox. She looks a little sad and tells me how last night in their living room she said, "Junior, when did I get so old and fat?" To which he replied, "Jeez, I don't know." He just isn't one to waste words. I get the mail and head home on the boat in the pouring rain. As I steer through the storm I find myself afraid, imagining what Wendy would do to to me if I ever answered her like that.

At home I can't help but notice there are quite a few leaks today. The wind is blowing over thirty knots from the east and driving the water in, probably right *through* the roof I built. I try to convince Wendy that a good house just has to breathe. She says, "It's drowning I'm worried about." I explain how it makes me feel as if I'm weathering a storm at sea. She says, "It makes me feel like I'm weathering a storm too, and it's in my kitchen!"

By four-thirty it's dark. The rain and wind have stopped. The coffee has left me in a slump. I pour two buckets of overflow water I left on the woodstove into the bathtub, the second bath of mine ever out here, and settle in to soak. The tub paint begins to peel. I put my head underwater and hum "Amazing Grace," with harmonies only the inside of a tub can give me.

Wendy and I argue briefly—I think it's something about a laundry bag (I enter best into the spirit of an argument and often do not pay attention to the content). Wendy storms out the door yelling, "Fine, I'm leaving you," then comes back in and tells me, "No, I'm not running away! I'm gonna stay around to cause you perpetual hell on earth!" She says I'm frustrated at her about something and why won't I talk about it? I yell, "I'm getting old and fat and bald and don't have a job and don't get to prove that I'm a man anymore by screwing lots of women and these are all complaints between my pity-ass victim self and God, so stop trying to take the fucking blame!" She smiles, my outburst being what she was apparently after from the start. Damn, outsmarted again! Why is it I'm so unable to outargue this girl?

DAY 171

The pine floor continues to dry and separate. The lumber must have been not quite twenty minutes old when it was delivered. Though we built it tight and solid, the "tongue-and-groove" boards are now a half inch apart. Not fall-through cracks, but see-through. I find this convenient for sweeping but Stephan, who lives downstairs, complains.

DAY 172

Totally white ocean with big surging waves, foam flying off the tips and an evil dark mist. The windows fog up and our world gets small, very small. From miles of open to no more than twelve feet in any direction.

Wendy's baking cookies. This means that the moon is about full and she's doing that weird girl thing again. She also bursts into tears for no reason and needs extra hugging at night. I'm liking her more and more. I find myself with teenager stomach love bubbles sometimes.

I'm only just now, in my Neanderthal way, realizing that Wendy is the center of all our lives out here. I can't even pretend to be more important. Stephan needs her for loving, games, and small things like room cleaning and motherly services. I just like to be near her. The dogs are worse. They follow her downstairs and watch her sweep, change, or go to the bathroom, insisting on going into the bathroom with her. All eyes are on her. Quite something, considering my belief that I am why the sun bothers to rise in the morning. At first I could joke about how if she dies I'll get that Humvee to replace her. Now that's not even funny; my feelings are deepening, uncomfortable for me and obviously good.

DAY 173

Now, here is a problem most people never get to deal with. Imagine a solid-as-ice block of shit three feet by two feet by two feet. That's twelve square feet. The buried thirty-five-gallon drum under the house filled up, and so the last few flushes sat in the pipe between the floor and the dirt and froze. As I hammered away, the pipe separated from the toilet, and about two gallons of exceptionally foul, not quite frozen stuff rained *through* the bathroom floor onto me beneath it, hammer clenched tightly as I felt chunks drizzle about me.

Being an optimist when bizarre things occur, I immediately thought (lied to myself) about how well I'd planned out making the toilet-room floor not waterproof, thus allowing proper drainage. As the sewage began to freeze my clothing and hair rigid I thought, "Oh good, *an igloo,* that'll keep the wind out."

Sailboats really have the best toilets for adventure. On an old family boat I remember, I pumped a clogged toilet until enough pressure built up for the expected *kerblam* of what I thought was the clog passing from the pipe to the sea via the through-hull fitting. Only during the next week did I notice a bad smell in the bilge, into which it turned out I'd been pumping everything. Uncovering the bottom of the canned-food bin I found the torn hose just where it went into the through hull. The initial clog, packed like a brick, was all that had kept us from sinking.

Years later I was sailing aboard *The Bill of Rights,* a 128-foot schooner and school ship I worked on. I was helping the guilty toilet-clogging student (discovered after a brief trial of twenty-seven "I didn't do it"s, with one abstention). This toilet blew all over me and the kid. He was wearing a raincoat, and I was still laughing at him for his "shit phobia" when the fluid shot all over my face and body.

The real highlight of today's adventure was losing my temper and with a .30-30 Winchester applying a rather aggressive pipe-unclogging technique. As the smoke cleared, I surveyed the damage. Essentially no more pipe . . . but I'm not easily discouraged, and with ringing in my ears, I duct-taped the shit out of it (actually, I duct-taped quite a bit of shit into it). Right in the middle of this Wendy yelled, "I have to use the toilet right now, it's an emergency!"

I had to empty the holding tank, leading to my current dilemma of what to do with this mass of frozen shit. It is like an entity—I really want to just "let it go," you know —a "live release" or something, like in *Born Free*. I have till April before it thaws and smells real bad, but still. It sits in the yard and I'm afraid to go out. Through the window I see Abby working on it like a cow on a salt lick.

10. Trouble in Paradise

Men are generally still a little afraid of the dark,
though the witches are all hung, and Christianity
and candles have been introduced.

— THOREAU

DAY 174

What a night. Our two main batteries are overfull of power, as the wind has been blowing forty-plus knots the last day. It's a good opportunity to get all the batteries charged, so I carried the boat ramp's battery from where it had died pulling the boat just halfway up. The solar charger is small and has trouble keeping the battery as charged as, say, a car would. These are big and heavy deep-cycle marine batteries, and I complained loudly while carrying the ramp battery between the harbor and the house ("Mom never told me where all the roots were" came to mind as the best excuse). I hooked it directly to the charger, topped off all the cells with water, and went to sleep blissfully happy knowing the wind was charging my battery. I sleep lightly when it's storming— from my sailing days.

I dreamed of dripping sounds: lava, waterfalls, and leaking roof, as I recall. Finally I woke up and still could hear dripping. In a space like this you learn all the sounds —like those from an expanding stovepipe, a draining sink, a cup blowing across the porch. This was a new sound.

It turned out to be hydrochloric acid boiling out the top of the overfull, overcharging battery. It went through the floor and onto the tool area, soaking my chain saw and collecting in a bucket of galvanized screws (which turned black and now, eight hours later, are rusty). So there I was at four A.M. mopping up battery acid. My knees burned and I looked down to see them peeking through my dissolving long underwear. Then my fingers burned and I saw bubbles in my newest wounds (a daily event here, collecting small wounds). Things got more painful by the moment, and I didn't know whether to cut bait or pray for a meteorite to hit me in the back and put me out of my misery. By then sparks were igniting on the terminals and I vaguely remembered how a warning on the plastic lids I'd removed earlier to add the water mentioned the words *vapor* and *explosion* in the same short sentence. A piece of fabric fell from my leg and a wisp of smoke curled from it and I was melting like the witch in *The Wizard of Oz*. My portable voltage meter was lying in a shallow pool of acid, and it began flashing signals and bleeping in a wounded way, as if to say that this particular activity was not within its specified parameters. I reached out just as a final burble of sound sighed from it. I thought "I've lost R2!" And then I screamed as something rubbed my leg. It was just Abby, curious. She left footprints, which smoldered, and as I watched she began moving quickly, a sort of erratic hopping dance, the point of which was to keep all of her legs in the air at the same time.

Well, I'd had it. Sparks, acid, wounds, burning knees, a dying electronic device, and a dog about to ignite. Feeling very much like a Monty Python character yelling, "Run away, run away!" I bounded down the stairs with Abby tangled and falling on me the whole way. I yanked the door open and leapt into the near-frozen mud by the woodpile. I wobbled on my knees and plunged fingers into the ooze as Abby ran circles. The water cooled our burns.

So here it is about five in the morning and I've worked up a sweat, am lying in the mud, wet, and trying to remember if the word is *hyperthermia* or *hypothermia*. Abby licks at the slightly thawing block and then my face.

DAY 175

Stephan finished his combined geography and history final and got an overall A−. We did some celebratory yelling and hollering, then got a good start on science.

I often wonder what it is I enjoy so much about teaching Stephan. When it's a subject I am passionate about, like science, I almost feel as if I can take a tiny bit of credit for all the miracles I am revealing to him. Like maybe I was the one who first figured it out, that I have inside knowledge to the secrets of life. There is magic in being right there with him when an idea really takes hold, when either an old belief crumbles or a new idea fills a previously vacant part of his awareness—that is a moment of creation, and I just love being the witness. For example, discussing plate tectonics is interesting, but cutting out all the continents and making your own assembled puzzle of the earth millions of years ago—the significance of that one little act is tremendous! It explains how mountains form, it turns the earth and all rocks into things that flow, it explains the floor of the ocean, and, most of all, it flips your whole perception of time on end. I have Stephan write a paper called "If I Were Patient Enough to Watch the Earth for Three Hundred Million Years."

On a day like this, I am giving, not teaching. There is no effort, no struggle, no moaning or complaining. Stephan is wide-eyed and alive, and so am I.

Fresh rye bread, red sunset. Seas still a froth, wind down to ten to twenty knots. Just an excellent place and an excellent family to be part of.

DAY 176

Beautiful clear afternoon, exciting ice-hockey game on the pond, with Abby sprawling about like a drunk sea pup.

On the radio we hear a story about using jackhammers to dig graves for a funeral to the north.

Cleaning up after dinner, I carefully sweep table crumbs into my hand as Wendy watches approvingly. She turns and I quickly dump them onto Abby, who I can always count on to move erratically and distribute the crumbs evenly. Wendy has somehow seen this and I quickly move in to hug her before she can get angry—an offensive defense, but I'm too late.

"You only *pretend* to be sensitive."

"Yes, honey, that's true, but would you prefer I was insensitive pretending to be sensitive rather than being insensitive and . . . "

"Don't talk. Just don't talk."

And thus our marital bliss is yet again saved from the gummy jaws of communication by Wendy telling me just how and when to shut up.

The moon was full a few nights ago and the tide was more than a foot lower than is common. I walked out in our harbor and jumped on the rocks I usually hit with the boat. I remembered my favorite picture book, where these seven identical-looking Chinese brothers each have special qualities. One of them can inhale the ocean and hold it in his mouth. In a picture he's doing this and the sea bottom is shown with all its miracles revealed, things always there but covered. I don't remember what the other brothers do, or finally what happens, but I will always remember the ocean's floor revealed and all the wonder of a "normal" thing uncovered. Would that we could all for just a moment see each other suchly.

Wendy

I carefully spoke to Daniel about maybe living in New Hampshire and getting a job at his old boarding school. We shall see what happens.

My head is busy getting ready for the future.

DAY 177

Wendy says I am "a gob of wounds who leaves blood around the house," the intensity of which is proportional to the number of tools I use on each project.

> Dear God,
>
> Just one flaw I've noticed—and that's not bad, considering. It's with girls. I think given how they become so dangerous to live with each month, what about giving guys a way to know. Maybe their hair could be on fire, or a high-pitched wailing siren could go off, or perhaps a big frog would hover over them and wave at us—*anything,* just please, *some warning!!!*
>
> Besides that, I'm pretty happy.
>
> Thanks,
>
> Daniel

DAY 178

The house is absolutely too small today. The inside of the windows are a sheet of ice, so there is nowhere else to gaze at, and Stephan is being a constant whiner. That is all the reason I need to go get the mail, so I am off in too rough a sea. Some really scared moments in big waves by the harbor mouth. The surges of ocean are fantastic— like a moving small mountain. Between the peaks are the troughs, and these are as spectacular as the foaming crests for simply being an empty space where one should not be: mountains of water hover on either side and the moment is underlined; you are aware it will not last, a perfect pregnant pause. I look down at the base of a trailer-sized rock we call Motu Kau Kau. It is like seeing your mother's underpants—it should never be! The whole harbor mouth is confusion. The aluminum boat is light, so I can leap out of the way or charge down and follow a particularly big wave, screaming and such in an attempt to keep it fun and deny the fear.

My version of doing doughnuts in the parking lot when I was a teenager was chasing after the Fishers Island ferry in the Thames River, in Connecticut. Her name was the *Olinda,* and what a beast she was, shaped like a forty-six triple-D. Following her in a speedboat was like trying to get a peek and not get slapped. She picked up speed just in front of our summer home—the one my father and I built when I was sixteen—and she would set up a standing wave six feet high. The crest of this wave would move with her at ten to fifteen miles an hour, and the game was to position yourself just falling off the crest of the wave and surf. If I went too slow, no problem, I would just wallow as the wave went under me. But if I went too fast I would lose control, hit the trough, and plunge into the bottom of the next wave, stopping too suddenly. The idea was not to die, with a little *style* if possible. Over the years, I got good at it and could ride the wave perched high and looking down on the faces of the passengers—the children anyway. Grown-ups tended to look away.

I wonder what mischief Stephan will get into during the tumultuous years ahead. Will he survive to raise his own brood? The life led in cities scares me. If I had stayed in New York for my adolescence I think I would have been killed from drugs, gangs, a car, or in any number of pointless ways. Stephan is safe here. Let him wander with his machete, get stung by giant mosquitoes, and get lost in the dark of the island's forest.

DAY 184—JANUARY

It blew so hard last night that Wendy and I both dreamed the house was picked up, like in *The Wizard of Oz*. I wasn't expecting this much of a blow, so I had left the windmill untied. It was howling like a pissed-off tiger. We both stared at the ceiling for a while, and then I put on a jacket, went outside, and approached the furious beast. A white glow at the top of an easy-to-climb spruce tree. The direction booklet has many warnings about just this sort of thing. It says the blade tips can travel at over three hundred miles per hour. There is no on/off switch. Lying nearby was a long stick, which I had purposely left there a week ago, anticipating just this situation. I picked it up and went to the back, sheltered side of the tree. The windmill's tail was now overhead—the blades faced into the wind—and I reached upward with the stick, thinking about the scene from the movie *Catch-22* where an airplane flies into a man and neatly cuts him in two.

By pressing the stick on the tail, I was able to spin the whole windmill 180 degrees. The blades quickly stopped, and before they could begin to spin the wrong way, I scurried up the tree and grabbed them. I pulled some rope from a pocket, lashed the blades to the tree, and was almost blown into the forest by a strong gust. Another exhilarating four A.M. adventure!

Back inside I saw the how large the seas were, from the southeast. At dawn the wind suddenly shifted to the west, shredding off the tops of the waves. It was brilliant to witness this as the red light from the rising sun hit and electrified the spray. Dazzling.

Stephan read *Shōgun* until three A.M.! I am so proud of him. I pray that no matter how I screw up, his love of books will save him.

Beautiful walk around the island with the girl. There is almost continuous surf from our harbor to Strawberry, a neighboring island two miles away. We found a big lobster claw washed up. It smelled fresh, so it became lunch.

DAY 190

I think the single most difficult thing in my relationship with Wendy is our different understanding of time. I like now, and Wendy likes to plan.

I am happy to have absolutely no plans. Wendy is panicked: What will we do? I avoid this as long as possible — just sensing that she is thinking about this makes me sleepy. Today she corners me:

WENDY: Daniel, I know it's just January, but we —
DAN: Hey, honey, what's for lunch?
WENDY: Daniel, we need to talk about this. What —

DAN: Look! An eagle!! I thought they migrated or something.

WENDY: We agreed, before we left, that this adventure would last one year. *One year.* That means that on July sixth—

DAN: I don't remember actually agreeing to *one year,* honey. I thought we sort of left that open, like—

WENDY: No, we said *one year.*

DAN: But aren't you—I mean, *why?* Give me one good reason!

WENDY (pulls a list out of her pocket!): I'll give you ten.

(She clears her throat, and reads:)

Reasons That We Have to Go Back to the Real World:

1. We will be out of money very soon.

2. Stephan needs to be around other human beings besides you and me.

3. I want to be able to step out my door and go jogging. I am getting tired of slipping on the ice, the seaweed, the slimy rocks, and the mud.

4. The *one* yard sale we went to absolutely sucked.

5. *Latte!*

6. I need a girlfriend I can talk to whenever I want, not just when I can get you to bring me ashore.

7. Fresh milk.

8. I like dressing up sexy sometimes.

9. *Baths!*

10. I am going absolutely crazy and may have to kill you soon.

There is a pause as I gather myself for rebuttal. The pause goes on a little longer than it should have before I reply: *"There's nothing wrong with canned milk!"*

DAY 191

Calm ocean, and it's a warm foggy day. We pack up and take the boat northeast to a small nearby island's harbor, hidden by a narrow opening—really a strange secret place where you would expect to see dinosaurs. There are clean white sandy beaches surrounded by impenetrable spruce thickets. The dogs run in circles of bliss as I wander off with an old borrowed shotgun.

I see a swimming duck, and since Wendy and Stephan are just over the little hill and can't see me, I figure it's okay to shoot it in the water and then make up a great story about how good a shot I am . . . so *blam,* I shoot at it. It's about my third time shooting a big shotgun. First I think, "Ouch, that hurts!" (It's like being punched in the armpit.) Then I notice that not only is the duck alive, but it hasn't even taken off.

Now it is swimming at me as if it knows I'm a New Yorker and could only be offering it bread crusts in the pond by the Alice in Wonderland statue in Central Park. Fear. I let fly another cloud of pellets, and I can't believe it—he is still coming right for me. I am disgusted, of course, but also a little scared. I have only seven more shells with me. I'm sure there are other ducks nearby, and before they can all start laughing I take the bold step of saying (lying to myself), "I'm feeling gracious today, so I grant thee, oh duck, life. Go prosper, live." I climb the hill (looking anxiously over my shoulder) and have a chicken salad sandwich . . . which I masticate with extra ferocity.

DAY 193

I've given up on trying to fix any more of the leaks in my house. I do not see this as a sign of cabin-fever apathy tightening its throat hold on me so much as a triumph for higher levels of justification. In the winter the wind blows so hard that the water has no trouble going up and under a six-inch weatherboard or even, over time, soaking into and through some one-inch pine. Anyway, the wavy stain patterns look great on the inside sills and dripping down the walls. This is such a relief, because I didn't know how I'd *ever* finish those walls with such an interesting pattern. So when it's blowing and the water level inside rises I don't feel guilty; I just call it art.

DAY 196

Stormy house shaking night but we are comfortable within foggy windows showing only what you draw on them.

Wendy can go from a loving cozy woman to a dangerous bison in 1.5 seconds, and when you suddenly find yourself in bed with an angry bison you are in trouble. There was this foam pad Stephan used as a mattress, which due to some leaks (art! I mean art!), got wet and smelly over time. Wendy was gleeful at having routed out the foul stench emanating from Stephan ("He's just a kid" was my explanation) and she wanted the pad burned. I figure anything you've carried out to an island is valuable and thus salvageable, so I hung it up on our clothesline. For two weeks it was rained on, snowed on, frozen, thawed, and flapped in the wind. Then I turned it over, and the same went on for another two weeks. I kept insisting it was *saved,* ("Call your mother!") but Wendy refused to let it back in the house.

Then she and Stephan went ashore for the night to Peter and Mary Ellen's, and so I remade our bed; it was now sporting the refreshed foam covered with the sheets.

The next night I've forgotten as we snuggle into bed and blow out our candles to watch the full moon. There are about five seconds of that wonderful sexy calm you share with someone you really like and then, as if all the balloons at the National Republican Convention have been dropped down into the crowd, all hell breaks loose.

First her body goes rigid and launches her, somehow, to a standing position next to the bed. Pure terror sets every one of my strained back muscles quivering at its own unique frequency. I fall off my side of the bed and hit the floor as Wendy runs around to a chair to grab and pull on her pajama bottoms while hissing, "No way, that is it, I'm out of here." Being on the floor as I was—and quite unable to move—I reflected on what was driving my wife to put on her pajama bottoms before really laying into me.

I couldn't help myself. I giggled.

When I regained consciousness I was just able to see Wendy hurling pillows and blankets in all directions. She was like a wood chipper running at ninety thousand rpms. In one swift motion she uncovered the slightly musty foam and flung it through the porch door into the gale of wind, which *moments* before had been rocking us to sleep.

The mattress opened like a parachute, and my last sight of it was a swirling shape skipping over the treetops, getting smaller as it leapt deeper into the unexplored forest to the north.

DAY 199

Brilliant sunup, way cold. Pancakes and an hour of quiet before Stephan wakes up. His slogan this week is "Do I have to?" Is the child suffering the early symptoms of a horrible illness called teenagerhood? Do we just keep feeding it and hope for the best?

Stephan usually makes a lot of noise in the morning. He clomps heavily up the stairs, maybe to warn us. But sometimes there's no sound at all and the hair on the back of my neck slowly rises, and I turn to see his grinning face peeking from under the whalebone banister.

After good mornings are exchanged he eyes the kitchen. Have we left him anything? Usually we have: some scrambled eggs, hot cereal, or maybe some steaming coffeecake Wendy just took out of the oven. Today he slathers a cold pancake with syrup and peanut butter.

Wendy and I usually awake with the sun, hours earlier.

Stephan reads, sometimes till three A.M., and he wakes when he is rested. He is less grumpy too.

I see his arrival upstairs as the half-hour bell for school. In the fishing shed, our schoolroom, Stephan sits at the table. Alas, there is only one chair, so I lie on the bunk, usually with a blanket over my feet. His home-schooling book is set up so that he goes along at his own pace. We talk about each section he completes. I want to be sure that what he is being exposed to is not an opinion disguised as history.

I get into trouble when he has math to do and asks me for help. Nine out of ten times my "help" is wrong. Luckily Stephan is gifted with enthusiasm. He has also been picking up some self-righteousness from me, so I have him back up in the book and teach me until we get to the question we are stuck on. I will argue my antiquated technique until he has to convince me that his way works better. In doing so he generally solves the problem. The other times I find myself saying, "Stephan, there will never be a practical application in your lifetime for this particular problem. Let's skip it."

Sometimes Wendy brings us lunch, maybe a tuna-fish sandwich. Usually we head to the house, the walk through the woods acting as a cleansing break. Today Wendy has made us tomato soup. An hour or so later we are back to work. If you've ever broken off the wooden handle on a lit bottle rocket you have some idea of how Stephan's mind works: spinning all over with showers of sparks. I have to pay attention to keep feeding the fire. It's a dance.

By three or four o'clock we are finished. I like doing this at a natural place in his lessons, say when he finishes chapter 7. Beginning another section because we still have fifteen minutes somehow seems disrespectful to his natural learning rhythm.

It's goof time till dinner. Stephan joins Wendy and me for a walk around the island, reads, or just runs off into the forest with his machete, quite happy. We blow a sort of foghorn at dinnertime if he's not back. I used to play the trumpet, so I can make a number of objects musical. Today I use a lobster buoy and get two notes. In the distance we can see and hear treetops rustling. I love to watch this—the commotion in the forest, the birds shrieking away in terror, the dogs barking—and then a scratched-up child with torn clothing emerges. He's usually hungry.

After a dinner of Oh My Gosh, Garlic (it's okay to name it once it's on the table), we play a game of cards or Monopoly. I am happiest when whatever Stephan is reading has got his attention so much that he gulps down his food and gets into bed to read it. Right now he is loving *A Confederacy of Dunces.*

Wendy and I read by candlelight. Usually our eyes begin closing at about the same time. We blow out the lights, tug at each other until sufficiently entwined, murmur a "good night" toward Stephan, and sleep.

DAY 201

Another exciting mail run. Ice formed on our suits on the way back, and many ducks laughed at me as I shot hun-

dreds of little bullets at them, which they were unable
fly into. I got frustrated and stood up, yelling, *"I'm da
gerous, godamnit, you STUPID CANADIAN DUCKS.*

At home, first Wendy opens her *Health* magazine with
"Oh great, how thin do I have to be this month?" I get
note from my checkbook-order company saying I can't get
any more Star Trek Thirtieth Anniversary checks because
it's now been thirty-one years, but I will be receiving
"eight rotating scenes, showcasing the most sought-after
ships of Star Fleet . . . and to add to this incredible series,
the back of each check is printed with the exterior
schematic of the ship!!" Who says living on a deserted island in the middle of winter is no fun? We celebrate with
martinis, and Stephan opens one of his hoarded sodas.

DAY 202
We're really inventing humor here. Such as last night,
when Wendy was showering. She can be such a neat
freak, so Stephan and I dumped a bottle of very bright
green food dye in the shower-water tank. Suddenly realizing I would not receive an enthusiastic response, I
got scared. I ran downstairs before the green had quite
reached the showerhead and blew out all the candles. I
pretended to fumble for matches until she ran out of water and her shower was over.

Stephan summed up the situation quite well: "That
was really close. We almost died."

• • •

DAY 207

We are becoming a little crazy, getting on each other's nerves. And it's not even February yet. Howling winds, ice-covered windows, three people and two dogs in a fourteen-by-sixteen cabin.

We heard Stephan late last night wearing headphones and singing painfully off-key along with an old Bread CD. He does not shut up. "Mom, did you know I can't shuffle as well with gloves on . . . look. *Mom!* Look, I have a *tail.* Where's Abby? *Mom!* These batteries are lasting *forever.* . . . What time is it? Oh, I have a watch. . . . *Mom,* I have a watch on and I just asked you what time it is. . . . *Mom, Mom!*

I wish some days were only thirty seconds long.

DAY 208

Wendy can't help it. When she looks at furniture catalogs her eyes mist over. She utters meaningless phrases about soapstone counters, saffron arrangements, and cream-colored cabinets. I go to my catalog and dream of a three-year food supply.

Speaking of nesting, Stephan is having his first date. Her name is Erica, and she is the daughter Peter most wanted to be a boy. (It's her never-used BB gun that Peter gave to Stephan.) She and Stephan wander about the island nervously together. There is a lot of card playing, and then a big Monopoly game the four of us play together. It's nice because Stephan hasn't become embarrassed about Wendy and me yet. (We still have that phase of child rearing to look forward to.)

I poured a quarter cup of rainwater out of the laptop computer. After two hours on the woodstove it's working fine. *Macintosh rocks!*

I have a job interview next week at my old boarding school. I'm trying not to think about it.

Stephan

It was extremely foggy today. Daniel is on edge. I read all day long, and Mom made cinnamon rolls. I am reading *Animal Farm*. I miss Erica. I want to go back to Idaho.

DAY 209

Wendy and Erica ashore in the morning, Wendy to an *overnight Tupperware party!* We're at the eastern edge of the continent, and Tupperware has found her . . . I'm thinking maybe I should change my name and move.

When it is fully dark we sometimes light fifty candles and place them on the windowsills. The effect is magical. At eye level there is only one small area with a non-glass wall, so the windows are everywhere. They reflect the candles, and then one another, so we feel like we are looking out from the inside of a lighted Christmas tree. Our one radio station is playing Micmac (Native American) chanting, an hourlong droning drumbeat with one-syllable words, on and on, the drums going at around one beat per second, like a heart.

Today Stephan goes twice around the island, with breaks for push-ups and sit-ups! Perhaps he has a crush on Erica?

As Stephan's teacher, I often have an image of myself as the father bird happily vomiting knowledge directly into his upturned gullet. I recite some Kafka: "You cast about too much for outside help, especially from women. Don't you see that it isn't the right kind of help?"

This elicits absolutely no reaction.

He's acting very grown-up, as if we couldn't possibly understand the ordeals of living, and he's right, in a way. We are limited by the beast of having *already gone through that,* of thinking we know all about it. Sometimes I feel like one of the grown-ups in *The Little Prince* who can see the drawing shown them only as a hat, unable to notice that it is really an elephant inside of a boa constrictor.

11. Ashore

> I should not talk so much about myself if there were
> anybody else whom I knew as well. Unfortunately,
> I am confined to this theme by the narrowness
> of my experience.
>
> —THOREAU

DAY 214—FEBRUARY

My job interview is in New Hampshire, a two-day drive.
The position is for an English teacher and dorm head.
Stephan has an all-day interview at the local fancy day
school, and Wendy is house shopping. I think both of
them would love the East, but I am afraid of what ghosts
might awake to haunt me.

The dogs can sense something bad. Perhaps the word
kennel is not in their vocabulary, but the feeling of strange-
ness is already upon them.

After falling our way over the icy trail to the motorboat, we're a pretty wounded and bruised-up bunch as
we leave the island. Last night's icy rain seems to be saying, "Don't go!" The ride in is wet, and the spray forms
into ice on our float suits. We haul the boat way up the
ramp by Junior's dock, the car starts, and we're off.

I should have been paying attention to the early indications that we were all a bit island spaced. Without social interaction one tends to become awkward. I've often been cut off from others. I have been forty-two days alone at sea. But Wendy and Stephan seem confused and a little in shock.

Tipping is the first obvious clue to our incompetence; Wendy and I are perplexed. Is it 7 percent? Is that the tax? Or is it 4 percent in Idaho and 17 percent in Nova Scotia? Sales tax, income tax at 30 percent . . . ? We just can't come up with a figure at the restaurant. There is also the issue of converting value, as Canadian and U.S. currency are both in dollars. It is funny and nerve-racking. I end up asking the waitress, "Would four dollars be a good tip?"

We drive for hours, and then U.S. customs looms ahead. I know that when my passport is handed over and scanned the computer will show a warning. The agent will press a button, or nod at someone, or something secret, and another agent will show up and ask me to follow them and sit here and wait. Then in five minutes a third agent will appear with a printout and say, "Mr. Hays, are you in possession of any restricted animal products?" and I'll explain no, two sperm whales washed up on my beach eight years ago and I got mounds of bones and once when I was coming through customs with a rib to give a friend, an agent got all upset since sperm whales are endangered and I said, "Hey, I ain't no Ahab, do you think I kill whales?" and it wasn't funny, and he got more upset, and he took my bone and made an entry in the computer's International Poacher and Dealer of Endangered Species list, and me with a master's degree in environmental science from a total tree-hugging save-the-whales kind of school. So now I get to tell the whole story each time I come into the States. It takes an extra fifteen minutes and I plan on it. Sigh.

Another eight hours of driving and we arrive in New Hampshire. We sleep in the same hotel—the same *room* —that I used to sneak off campus to with my girlfriend. The ceiling once again swirls in LSD patterns, my first decent flashback in years.

In the morning Wendy dresses us. Stephan is nervous and changes four times. I'm in denial about being nervous and change five times. At eight o'clock Wendy drives us up the big hill (Stephan changes once more in the car) and drops her two men off for a day of terror while she shops.

My interview goes well except for when I casually mention how New Hampshire has no concealed-weapons permits, how anyone can carry a gun without any sort of background check. Why I would bring this up with the three liberal women interviewing me is yet another issue I will avoid going into therapy for. It just sort of lies on the table like a nude hippo until I brilliantly try to extricate the foot from my mouth with a sentence containing the word *acrost,* a word popular in trailer parks but not at a New England prep school English-teacher interview. I suppose I am moved by the spirit of my "got kicked out of this school twenty years ago" ghost past, because the next thing I hear myself saying is "Fuck, I can't hardly believe I just said that!" On an apparent roll, I go on with "Sorry, my English wavers." Then I just shut up, me and my herd of hippos, until Wendy comes to get me.

Wendy excitedly tells me about her day looking at houses. She found six we cannot afford. She also filled out lots of Stephan's paperwork, and left them a $9,500 deposit. After a very short pause I do the male version of a scream. It seems only thirty dollars was required as an application fee but she got "confused" and accidentally paid a year's tuition.

We pick up Stephan. He's red faced. After much coaxing he tells us how shortly after a trip to the bathroom a girl screamed at him and he found his penis was sort of showing, which happens on the island sometimes, but out there, so what?

We drive back to our island, our heads hung in social disgrace.

Ever since being arrested and deported at the Canadian border I continue to tense up when I get close. It's like buying beer and alcohol; to this day, as I approach the counter I begin to sweat. Pretty soon we are all tense. While we're in line with two cars ahead of us Stephan asks to play one of his CDs. We groan but comply. Suddenly Queen's "Fat Bottomed Girls" fills the car. I crank it up. The tension breaks and we all begin banging our heads with the beat. The customs man eyes us as we pull a car closer—I swear his eyes rotate so that one is on us, one on the car before him. When it's our turn I roll down the window and we just look at him, a bit bleary but bright-eyed. He waves us through. It is my easiest border crossing ever.

Wendy

I was very excited about Daniel's interview and also lots nervous. I wanted him to be perfect and say all the right things. I set up an interview with the local private junior high and it went off great. I was sitting in with the head of admissions and Stephan was checking out the library. Pretty soon the woman from the library passed by the door and peeked in to say what a wonderful polite kid Stephan was—boy, was I beaming.

I also went around with a realtor to look at some houses in the area, to get a feel for the market. I was very excited about the idea of moving. One of the houses I saw was 150 years old. It was a farmhouse, and there was a big old barn next to it. But the day was very nerve-racking, and by the time we had to go back out to the hotel and into traffic Daniel was ready to get the hell away from the East Coast.

DAY 218

All our hearts speed up as we drive the final miles to our bliss. We rescue the hounds from their purgatory. We visit Junior and Becky and are told not to go out. Sea ice is floating around Junior's dock, big sofa-sized chunks. It will be dark in under an hour and it is at least twenty degrees colder than I've ever experienced here. Even though I'm thinking "Hell, I'm thirty-nine, I'll do whatever I want," I recognize something in their weathered faces, something beyond having lived within fifty feet of these tides for over seventy years and knowing when to stay on dry land. My family has just been adopted.

In the past I've tried to impress Junior with stories of sailing around Cape Horn in a twenty-five-foot engineless sailboat ("Yeh? Where the hell's that?"), biting the head off a live rattlesnake ("That was stupid"), and even leaving his dock in a fog so thick that the moment I could see anything was the moment I had to swerve to avoid it ("It was nice knowing ya," he said, waving, as I left his dock). Maybe it's trying for a new dad's approval—Junior and my father were born the same year, and Peter and I were born the same year too. Maybe some psychological thing is going on, or maybe I just think too much. But even I can sense when to shut up, and we drive back many miles to an icebound hotel, appropriately named the Last Dive.

The next morning we bundle up with everything we have—we're even wearing heavy neoprene gloves. With nothing but nostrils showing, we push off the boat and head home. The strong north winds shove us along. As is our custom when returning after more than a day or two, we circle our small kingdom before landing. Blocks of ice are washed up, and because the last snowstorm came with a strong north wind, the snow has been packed onto the north side of everything. It is magical. From the south the island seems snowless—just spruce green everywhere. A quarter of a circle later, all seems in shadow like that feature available on most computer style menus. From the north we see only snow, a single bright-white shoreline pushing skyward past the trees.

Even Wendy breaks the eggs as we slither along our icy trail. The dogs romp in insatiable ecstasy, sometimes sliding ass first down hills, exhilarated by facing the wrong way and watching things get smaller as they accelerate.

The house is encased in ice and looks like the Winter Palace in *Doctor Zhivago*. With a log from our woodpile Stephan gently taps away at the ice until the door can move. We huddle around the stove as I light the pyramid of wood that I'd already prepared. (I always assume I will be returning near dead of cold, and rather than have to cut open a dog, wife, or child to crawl into for warmth, I leave the stove just a single match away from heating a whole family.)

Three bottles of Wendy's high-class drinking water have exploded from the cold. Two fifty-five-gallon blocks of ice hint at no running water for a while. The olive oil will not pour. But we're home and it's beautiful to our bones.

12. The Insanity of an Anatomy

> Sooner murder an infant in its cradle than nurse
> unacted desires.
>
> —BLAKE

DAY 224

I've been taking Prozac since I was thirty-five or so. I've had numerous discussions with the parents of the kids I've worked with: medicate or be natural? Or deal with the issues when medicated and *then* be natural? The bottom line for me is that taking Prozac allows me to focus on one thing at a time. I spent twenty years roving the planet for the perfect woman, the perfect drug, the perfect moment. My restlessness was insatiable. I was repeating the same behaviors again and again with little internal growth, automatically having to "change the channel" on life every few years. It was great for working with kids—I immediately had a rapport with them. But enough was enough.

Out here though, on this island, I've been weaning myself off the Prozac lately. It seems a safe place to experiment. I would like to not depend on a drug company. And the first quality of my old self to rear its head is constant horniness. This serves Wendy right, because she's been able to complain for two years about needing more sex and now I'm starting to hear "Oh no, not again," and it's music to my ears. I'm back in the saddle—no, I *am* the saddle, and it's a *Western* saddle, yahooey!!!

When I was twenty-six I went back to college to take pre–medical school classes and I was in the library a lot. I'd stolen a key to the airtight windows and so could sneak in (I had *great* sex one night on the main reference desk). Anyway, I would go so berserk hour after hour, leaving love letters to freshmen in their books when they weren't looking, drinking dozens of coffees a day, streaking, sneaking into the chapel at three A.M. and playing the really cool pipe organ, breaking into the power-plant building and turning off the entire campus's electricity . . .

Those were truly manic times. I went to a shrink who tried me on lithium, but that was plain old boring and I couldn't drink enough coffee to get manic again, so I stopped taking it. Then she shook her head in judgment at me one session as I raved over some sexual fantasy. So I quit. I hadn't even gotten to talking about what I wanted to do with her and a bucket of warm soapy water on the wing of a 747. Ten years later I saw her being interviewed on TV. I happened to be on a 747 and I gazed longingly out the window for the remainder of the flight —with the tray table down.

DAY 225

Last night I had a real hissy fit, and I'm thinking maybe I should take the Prozac again. There is an edge I experience in life, like a crick in my neck, that drives me into retreat, as if I'm better off all alone.

I'm thirty-nine. I've been in therapy. I've seen all the Woody Allen movies. I figure this must just be how I'm wired. I'm teeming with rebellious neurotransmitters. And sadly, I seem to be unbearable to my family without my Prozac. Especially at night, when I must turn on the radio so my thoughts can unfocus; otherwise they chug on and on, leaving fractal trails in multiple shades of black.

I am seeing the world as if looking through foggy goggles of despair. Reality is completely subjective. For people with big chemical imbalances, the world really *is* all screwed up. No wonder they are so unhappy. It amazes me that brain chemicals can shift all this, how perceptions of reality can be altered.

All week I've just floated in gloom and tension. The daily events in my life align with it—they actually seem to have a negative purpose, to be a breathing beast. I fight with Stephan; I back the boat into a rock, denting the prop; the toilet's holding tank is full; the weather gets foggy, stormy; the woodpile falls over; Wendy has vicious PMS. It's a laundry list of woes, and I created it all.

I've always been an enthusiastic participant in self-medication programs. I am a firm believer in Garrison Keillor's comment, "You can learn more about life by drinking gin straight from the bottle than you can by watching TV."

I had a great nostalgic episode a few days ago. I was in

the fishing shed listening to "Spirit in the Sky," "Magic Bus," and "Bad to the Bone." I had shots of tequila lined up, a loaded shotgun to make hell with, and I was young again, gonna stay up all night and bark, break stuff, spray-paint graffiti, the whole thing. So I gulped down four shots, one, two, three, and four, and then fell over and lay on the ground *dry retching*. My eyes were all teary, and the gun fell over and went off, and I crawled back to the house and went to sleep. I woke up the next morning no smarter and with a bad hangover. "If you want to really relax sometime, just fall to rock bottom and you'll be a happy man. Most all troubles come from having standards." —Thomas Berger

DAY 226
We woke to another half-inch ice sheet covering everything. The trees are beautiful, each outlined in pure sparkle. I stepped outside, just one step, and I slid thirty feet, till a tree stopped me with absolutely no grace. Stephan threw me the end of a rope and pulled me back. I really love it when something happens and I *need* him like that. It's good for me because I have trouble allowing him to help when I'm vulnerable, and it's good for him because I make a big deal of thanking him, letting him know that he's a good person, and that I love him. I wish didn't, but I seem to need excuses to do this.

It is twenty degrees and windy, one of those "tingling nose-hair cold days." Dangerous, it occurs to me. Maybe we should stay in for a few days? Strange squeaks and crackles fill the air as the house moves within its shell. Great Cream of Wheat and coffee.

Home-schooling Stephan continues to be a handful. His level of intellect oscillates between kindergarten and graduate school. Within a span of minutes I might say, "Stop chewing your eraser," "Don't put your finger in that," "A-N-T-H-R-O-P-O-M-O-R-P-H-I-C," "Seventeen and eleven-sixteenths," "Get back in here," "It was a nineteenth-century word for *depression*," "Stop blowing in the dog's nose," "Water molecules vibrate that way," "Combustion," "FeO_2," and "Yes, that's a big booger." Sometimes I'm frustrated but usually I am proud. His mind is hungry, and if I am helping to feed that, maybe it's worth all my complaining.

DAY 227

Now it's just ten degrees and windy, the fire barely warming us. I keep the stove full.

The following conversation best describes the tension between Wendy and me:

ME: Honey I want to discuss this. I've had to suppress it my whole life and I'm ready to talk: I think the world is going to end next winter, Y2K and all, and I want us to be here, where—

WENDY: That's a bunch of bullshit. You're just trying to get out of having a life, a job, and dealing with reality.

ME: So you want me to suppress this, stuff it back into the dark and let it slowly manifest itself in pimples, angst, and eventually cancer . . . ?

WENDY: You're so full of shit.

ME: Okay, but can we get ready at least? I'll need four thousand dollars for two years' worth of food. Three thousand dollars for lots of bullets and stuff, and I have to smuggle my guns here and—

WENDY: I am not staying here. Besides, we need money, income, you know?

ME: Honey, you are too caught up in what passes for life! You have to understand the apocalyptic magnitude of the year 2000, the . . . honey? Hey, Wendy! You're not listening!

(She licks Subway coupons and sticks them on the card they give you to fill up so you can get a free sub. I cannot think of anything that so symbolizes faith in the world's inevitable continuation.)

ME: Honey, just six thousand dollars . . . well, seven. We need two miles of barbed wire.

WENDY: Daniel, I'm *so done* with this conversation.

ME: Wait, come back! How about just one year's supply of food!? Honey? . . . *Wendy?*

DAY 228

I drove our boat through a quarter mile of slush ice to get to the mainland this morning. I was sent ashore by Wendy to pick up her just-arrived Tupperware; Junior called us on the radio to give us the news, so now it is public knowledge. Of all the things I wanted to avoid during this lifetime (not to mention this year, isolated in the Atlantic and all), this was one of them. I have failed.

So now I have Tupperware. At the party she won all these Tupperware prizes; the Tupperware lady shakes a bowl she's about to demonstrate (definition of culture: *demonstrating* a bowl), and if it rattles, and if you're the first woman to say "I love Tupperware!" the shaken item becomes your free gift. Wendy won them all. It is mid-February and I go across seven miles of stormy iceberg-infested Atlantic Ocean and through a quarter mile of slush ice for Wendy. Is this one of those times when she is afraid for my life, imploring me with sweet cries of "Don't go, honey, it's too dangerous"? No, this is not such a time.

I peek inside the package Junior has brought to the dock for me. I think it's a cheese grater and a serving pitcher. I look at them and I sigh.

DAY 230

Big storm last night, winds forty knots from the southeast for twelve hours. Huge seas. I took our movie camera, put it in its waterproof case, and went out on the point to film the fury. I was engulfed by icy water three times, and two times knocked over. I was washed up and sideways along the rocks. I was joined to the whole storm, I was water and air, bubbles and swirling currents, foam and power. I was free of all decision making. I was scared shitless. Luckily I was a little drunk, so I didn't mind the fear.

• • •

DAY 231

The whole harbor is frozen. Sheets of ice lifted and dropped by the tides are packed together. The wind has blown it all toward the shore, and it is too thick for us to even think of launching the boat. Stephan walks out to the middle—where it is maybe fifteen feet deep at low tide—and I take a picture of him dancing like John Travolta in *Saturday Night Fever*.

February drones on, and we continue to bother one another in numerous ways. I've been two weeks without Prozac. Waiting to hear if I got the job, if we'll be moving to New Hampshire or if I'm unemployed. Our savings are running out and I'm being reminded of Y2K on the radio, only ten months away, hearing how all hell will break loose.

I lock myself into my writing shed. It contains my short list of essentials: namely, a bottle of rum, pen, paper, and a sleeping bag.

I riffle through stacks of surplus and G.I. Joe wanna-be catalogs. A good catalog presents you with things you did not know you couldn't live without. (Good marketing strategy: elicit the lowest common denominator of all angst.) Thumbing through one, I come across an ad to buy gold coins, "The Final Protection." (A misprint in the ad claims, "GOD is trading just above its eighteen-year low, buy now.") In the classifieds, I find I can receive "FREE BOOKLETS: Life, Death, Soul, Resurrection, Pollution, Crises, Hell, Judgment Day, Restitution, Bible Standard . . ." What an offer, all for free. I could be normal and still become upset reading that ad.

Here is my favorite:

POLAR SHIFTS / ADJUSTMENTS HAVE
brought Tremendous changes To earth in
past ages. Imminent polar shift due To
Usher in Positive way of life for Positive survivors.
Prepare To Evacuate. For Special Report,
send Three first-class stamps To . . .

What the hell? It makes me even more afraid, 'cause I thought I knew what I was scared of and now I see there are fears I'm ignorant about! This adds a new depth to my paranoia. Perhaps I should start taking my Prozac again.

Or I could just buy this preassembled bomb shelter. The deluxe comes with a year's food, air, and water-purification equipment.

DAY 233

Half the firewood is used up, so we're letting the fire go out at night. Heavy fog all day, outside and in. Wendy is desperate for shore but it is way too rough, and a lot of ice is about. Hoping for calmer seas in the morning.

The best meal I've invented this year is burnt spaghetti. It is a leftover restorative that is unequaled. The only problem is that it is not so easy to make. Every instinctual cooking gene is personally violated, and one's common sense assaulted.

The thing is, it just cannot be done intentionally. You take leftover spaghetti and put it in a pan, over high heat, and then you need a distraction. The urge to stir is tremendous. A good thing might be to go prod the fire along, glue something, go search for a lost item behind a really big object—but even then when you return, it is too soon. Find another distraction. When you've done that, come back, flip the whole mess over like a pancake, and do all this again. And then, when you return, it's done, and good to feed to kids and dogs, although Wendy coincidentally begins a diet each time I make it.

Stephan seems at a critical developmental stage, the purpose of which is to convince us that we are doing pretty much everything wrong. Any requests from us either are met with a cry of incredulity or are endured with loud sighs. ("What?! I brushed them *last* night!) When he storms off to sulk he emits subsonic tones that seem to move inanimate objects like a cup toward the edge of a table, where it plummets to the floor. These objects are his allies. They give him evidence of a cruel world.

There are other stages of his growth that bewilder me. Recently he has begun using risky words out loud. Words that incite a sort of maniacal giggle. Topping this list is *fart*. We don't just get it a few times a day; when he is possessed by this demon we get it purely, barely connected to other words, as in, "Oh farted, I farted, fart fart farty fart." He calls Abby "Fart," so a monologue may sound like "Oh Fart, there you are, Fart, *Farty*, oh Fart Fart."

The kid is an infinitely deep well of enthusiasm. When I think of *Joy*, it is his beaming face I see.

DAY 236

Now Wendy is reading *The Three Musketeers* and I am told just what a lump of egg white I am compared to the

Duke of Buckingham. "He risked his life just to pronounce his love for the queen." Screw him—I'd prefer risking my life to having to pay phone bills and cut firewood and say "Yes, dear" thirty times a day. *Not* letting the dogs lick all the dishes clean because "it's disgusting"—that's *real* love, damnit. Anyway, I did risk my life for her Tupperware.

The existential implications of this are too much for me. I start taking my Prozac again.

DAY 238
When the rain barrels are full and the voltage is over 12.8, I am so happy.

DAY 240—MARCH
Big blowup in school; this kid can throw a fit. Later Stephan wrote a cool paper on it called:

MY FITS
by Stephan H.

What triggers my fits is when I get a question wrong on a test or I lose a game. It can also happen when somebody makes a correction about something I'm doing. This then makes me think I am stupid. Then my anger starts to boil. My brain is saying, "You're not stupid. He must be stupid. You're supposed to be perfect."

When I start to have a fit I go into "repel mode." I won't let anybody touch me. I make sudden jerky movements when anybody tries to touch me. I won't answer any questions and if I have to, it's in a monotone. I act like there is no one around me.

When I am at the peak of a fit I start yelling at people

or things. Then when I'm told to leave I storm away. This makes it their fault. Before I leave I'll do something physical, like upset a table or hit a wall.

When I cool down, after a little while I'll feel like I still want to destroy something, even though I've hit things. So when I am outside I'll break sticks against things and I'll tear off branches on trees. I try to stay away from people for a little while.

The benefit of having my fits is that I get to be right. When somebody else wins a game, they don't really get the satisfaction of winning. When I have a fit I get a lot of negative attention. Another benefit is that although I secretly "believe" that I'm stupid, I try really hard to prove to other people that I am not stupid. That is why I am an A student. (That's all pretty stupid, isn't it?)

The cost of having fits is people getting mad at me. I don't get the satisfaction of playing with somebody. If I had a girlfriend and I had a fit she would probably leave me for some other guy.

I think I learned this from my father [He means the ex, not me. —D.H.] because our fits are about the same. He has his because he thinks he is a bad person. I have mine because I think I'm stupid.

It's kind of how people believed the world was flat. The world was flat. I'm stupid only because I say so.

Well, so much for trying to outsmart the kid with all my fancy psychology! He is a smart rat, and truthfully, I feel a sense of pride. I like to think that I taught him some of that, gave him enough permission to look and laugh at how absurdly we construct our reality.

13. Angst

Wherever a man goes, men will pursue and paw him
with their dirty institutions, and, if they can, constrain
him to belong to their desperate odd-fellow society.

—THOREAU

DAY 241

I hated the idea of living on the East Coast. While waiting to find out about the prep school job, I had dozens of
turmoil-ridden dreams, the sort that Freud would be eager to laugh at. So I am relieved at the rejection letter, but
Wendy is heartbroken not to have a house in New Hampshire. I say, "Relax, babe, I'll get us a trailer," and I try to
comfort her by saying it would be "a trailer parked by a
silo with a big pipe connecting them—some corrugated
iron pipe like they put under roads. Then we could have
a cool spiraling stairway in either the center or along the
silo walls, windows, . . . and bale of straw for the floor
and rug! We can change it each week, and . . ." But she's
not listening anymore.

Actually, our next house has to be hers. She's had to
put up with nearly a year's worth of things like asking for

a bureau, then me finally dragging in a piece of driftwood and screwing it into the wall and saying, "Anything else?" She's had to put up with a whalebone-jaw sink, swimming creatures in our drinking water, a toilet that sometimes says no. So the next house will be hers. I would like to have just one room, my own war room. There I will be king, and I'll have a NO MARRIED GIRLS ALLOWED sign on the door.

Sometimes I feel pretty hopeless about this, our two living styles. What follows is an example of a real conversation.

WENDY: Honey, we have to buy a new bed for next year.

DAN: No, we don't. What's wrong with the old one in storage?

WENDY: You sold it with the house—a "bonus," you said.

DAN: No, I didn't.

WENDY: Yes, you did.

DAN: I don't remember that.

WENDY: You don't remember a lot.

DAN: Oh? Like what?

WENDY: Honey, we need a new bed.

DAN: No, we don't. What's wrong with the old one?

WENDY: . . . I'm buying a Hollywood frame for Stephan's mattress.

DAN: What's a Hollywood frame?

WENDY: A bed thing, it holds the mattress.

DAN: I'll make one—a piece of plywood, cinder blocks—

WENDY: No, I'm buying one. This will be my house!

DAN: Look, how about I nail the mattress onto the wall and we train Stephan to sleep leaning against it?

WENDY: Go to your garage and be quiet.

Wendy

When Daniel read me the letter I got very depressed. All I could think of was, Where is Daniel going to get a job, where are we going to get money, and where am I going to live?

DAY 242

It is still wintry, even more so because of the rain and storms. The wetness penetrates our clothes. We hide inside.

I watch ducks in a storm. They float maybe a hundred together—"rafting," it's called. They face into the wind and tread water just where the sea breaks onto the rocks. On the south side of the island, where the big seas come from, there are usually one or two of these rafts. This one is right in front of our house.

Storm-tossed is the phrase to best describe the scene. Each duck kicks into the wind, bobbing high sometimes just an inch from where the rolling wave begins its break. Every five minutes or so several bigger waves come together and this delicate surf line is moved into their midst. The ducks north of the surf line vanish, diving down and leaving a circular ripple, which is immediately devoured by a surge of foam. When the wave passes, heads followed by bodies cork to the surface. The water immediately rolls off them, and they appear quite unruffled.

They do this without pause. This storm blows from the south for eighteen hours. The seas grow to over ten feet where they pile up and fall over onto the rocks. The ducks keep going, hour after hour, hovering inches from the breaking point.

DAY 243

It has been gray and stormy all week and it's only faith that lets me know there is a sun, a moon, and a mainland nearby. The radio tells me there is a Canada—well, a Nova Scotia anyway—but overall, with the fog outside and inside our windows, the world is quite small and entertainment is scarce.

Yesterday occurred the three most amazing sneezes of the year. I was walking past Bear and I noticed one of his eyes closed, and the other trembling as if he were a drunk trying to recover from a fall. His head was tilted at an odd angle and I was alarmed. Suddenly a sneeze erupted. The sneeze's intensity arose not so much from its volume as from its shortness—a perhaps full second's worth of a hurricane's fury condensed into a frightful fraction of a moment. It was spectacular.

Bear repeated this twice more. His expression between was one of an exasperated drunk during an epileptic fit. We all clapped as the final cloud of mist settled on the nearby alarmed Abby. When he was through we gave him many pats of approval. Entertainment is valued on Whale Island.

The second amazing event of the day was Stephan's first hands-on experience with what lies at the bottom of the toilet's drainpipe. Just as darkness was falling the child crept upstairs and confessed to having lost control of the shit poker, a three-foot-long dowel. When not poking poop down the pipe, the bottom end of the poker lives in a bottle with an inch of Clorox. Armed with a flashlight we crawled under the toilet room and peered down the mysterious tunnel, and sure enough, there it was. "Don't worry, Stephan," I said, "the rescue is easy. All I have to do is aim the flashlight and give you orders!" He was initially horrified. What better time, he asked, for a dad to be a dad than when reaching into a septic tank?

"This will be a great learning experience, for you," I replied sternly.

This turned out to be one of my proudest moments. With only a small sigh, Stephan dove into the job, both hands deep, and performed a flawless extraction. More than anything, being a man is doing what must be done, and doing it with some dignity. Stephan may have sensed the importance of this bar mitzvah–esque moment. He even asked for a hug, which I declined, pointing him toward the shower.

DAY 245

I dreamed I met God last night. I stepped from the stoop of my childhood archenemy's brownstone on the West Side into purgatory. It was a TV version of an Old West mining town, and there was no escape. When I tried to retrace my steps, the way was blocked by a river, or a stampede, or a bunch of old men in rocking chairs. I had friends there, and we were all looking to escape, but we knew it was a personal thing that would let you out, not a hidden door we could share with one another.

I gave up anything that I thought was the right way out. I became free of my mind and just leapt from a roof, figuring that, as in a dream, *things would work out.* As I fell a seagull flew over me and I hung on to its legs. We flew across the street and I was let go on a roof—the kind that some bad guy always gets shot off of.

That's when I talked with God, a loving and thoroughly understanding being in the guise of my grandmother. I was quick at dispensing with any excuses; she spoke directly into my heart. My problem came down to having missed an opportunity and how I would now have regrets. I was guilty of mediocrity and had to go back to West Eighty-sixth Street and face my enemy. I could no longer hide behind being a grown-up. I cried, and we embraced. It was wonderful to hug my grandmother again, after all the years since she'd died. As I was leaving I saw God transform into a large old black woman, and a skinny black man who'd been waiting in line behind me was reaching out, in tears, to hug her.

DAY 246

Wendy's been trying to talk to me all day about the future. Now that my old high school said no to hiring me, we have no plans at all for after the thaw. She feels unsettled. I just don't want to deal with it.

"You're gonna get a job," she says. I'm brushing my

teeth as she utters these horrifying words and I somehow snap my toothbrush, and then I'm bleeding inside my mouth, with the taste of iron. Even as I write this she's peering at me, saying, "Tell me when you're done with that. I want to discuss next year." Panic! I just want to do emergency *right now* things, anything but discuss the future. As a matter of fact, I can't think of anything more revolting. So I make my *now job* to avoid the topic and stay pleasantly occupied. I claim to have a headache, I have to go the bathroom, and finally: "Dear, I took a sleeping pill and it just hit me and I'll be happy to talk with you but it will be incoherent and you don't want that, do you? This is important, I should be awake." I fake sleep till her light snores allow me turn on my flashlight and read under the covers.

I've always found myself flowing into continuous moments of *right nows*. I do the best I can with each now that I find myself in. I'll deal with the future when it becomes a now, and not a moment sooner. I truly believe that in this area men and women are wired completely differently. I can fix a flat tire. Wendy can plan a wedding. Maybe I am emotionally undeveloped, just a child in the ways of forethought, an evolutionary throwback on par with jellyfish. Maybe I should write a book called *The Attention Deficit Disorder Association's Book of Wild Animals of North Amer—Hey! Let's Go Ride Our Bikes!*

• • •

DAY 247

Wendy and I have a date. We deposit Stephan at Peter's home, where he will have the thrill and terror of being with Peter's twelve-, fourteen-, and seventeen-year-old girls. We leave him quaking on the porch, all three girls inside wearing boxers and T-shirts. I can hardly imagine, after months on an island with just his parents, the percent of fear and young testosterone in his veins. "Good luck," I say. "Stay calm, pretend to be thoughtful. That's what I do."

We go to a hotel. We've brought an avocado, chips, a bottle of rum and are planning, if all goes well, to attempt a sexual encounter. What with Stephan living just a few boards away . . .

DAY 248

Home by sunset. Stephan seems all right, though quiet.

DAY 249

Strong south winds at forty to fifty knots. I slept uneasily, as I would at sea, and at sunrise we woke up to a loud *smack* as quite a bit of ocean hit the windows. Wendy and I sat bolt upright, the sound being very much in the "I never heard that before" category. Nothing broke, and I am thankful to be behind glass to watch this one. The rocks off the house are all white in mist—a strange illusion, as if you can't focus on them. The waves are so big that the rocks seem small—as if they moved further out during the night.

There is a taste of salt water in the southern drinking-water tank. Some wave must have made it to the roof! Our fillet knife, whose point is wedged between two beams, vibrates faster and faster with the gusts. Both dogs curl up by me, the house shuddering.

In the evening the three of us play a drawn-out game of progressive rummy. It's drawn out because Stephan chose the music, the *Star Trek* sound-effects CD . . . so I'm looking for a pair of fours while listening to five solid minutes of *bridge sounds,* searching for spades during two minutes of *door opening and closing sounds,* and I lose the hand as *photon torpedoes* are being fired.

DAY 254

On our walks Wendy often relieves tension by running to each and every sea urchin a gull has left on the rocks. She stomps them for that satisfying crunch they make, like bubble wrap. Abby is a little distressed by this, because she loves to eat and later vomit these same urchins. Abby is faster than Wendy but is easily distracted, so they're usually neck and neck.

I've already mentioned the tragedy of dogs not having pockets, and seeing Abby is almost painful; she just loves *things*. On today's walk, just fifty feet from the house she finds the perfect stick. It's two feet long and old enough to get a good bite into. She holds one end and runs by Bear, enticing him to grab the other end. Many of our walks begin with the two dogs jaw-locked this way, charging full speed down the trail, heads oddly in perfect step together. But today Bear won't be tempted. She brushes by several times and turning, seems to say, "Hey, this really is the *best stick out here*—you better come get some or it's all mine." He doesn't, so with a sad look in her eyes she walks behind us, the stick scraping the rocks and pulling her head to the side as it snags on roots and rocks.

This is the tragedy of not having a pocket. There is a good eighth mile of boulder-jumping shoreline ahead. Indecision.

She follows with the stick, struggling along lopsided. It's warmer today and I know she has to pant, her tongue dying to be set free.

Wendy and I root for her. I don't think she's smart enough to have the concept of getting the stick over this section of island to the dock. If she makes it that far the stick will be safe, in an area she often visits. Wendy thinks she'll make it. We can't cheer out loud because we know it would distract her into a smile and she would forget about the stick.

Halfway and we start to choose all the easier paths, Abby a step behind—though often in the same step.

The final beach, and *she makes it.* The stick is carefully laid in a hole she's dug to sleep in while waiting for the boat (and us) to return after a laundry or food run. Her tongue leaps out, does a thorough once-over her acre and a half of lips, and she smiles, running after us, continuing on our tour. She does her most joyous thing, a sort of front-to-back waddle while holding her back rigid, much the same as a happy llama might do. She's free of needing a pocket, and the world becomes perfect again.

And that is what I want, to be caught up in a series of wonderful right-now moments. Wendy is upset at me about something intangible, a later-than-now moment. It's intangible to me, anyway. If I ever fall off a really high cliff, I'm going to enjoy the gravity, not flap my arms.

14. Storms

> Only to the extent that man exposes himself over
> and over again to annihilation, can that which is
> indestructible arise within him.
> —KARLFRIED GRAF VON DÜRCKHEIM

DAY 261

Yesterday afternoon there was a scent in the air, a primitive thing . . . I was able to sit back and let Stephan drive the boat with only a couple of encouraging suggestions, like "Isn't that land?" and "*Either* side of that," but still, they were positive. I remembered that I love him and am proud of him. I let him be twelve. I think the best gift you can give to anyone is to see and love them as they are. Simple acceptance—it is what we spend so much of our lives running in circles for.

Today I take the boat out alone, and as I'm riding over the waves, surfing up and down ocean swells, I am seized with the desire to simply head away from the shore. Forget my family, forget anything that holds me to the land. The water is blue and soothing and spreads before me unlimited, potential without encumbrance. I'm standing in

the boat holding the tiller, knees bent. A living thing, me
and the boat. I lean one way, feel the bow coming down,
lean the other way. I steer just with my body. I look into
the splash I've made—forty feet on either side, and a
sheet of spray ahead, which I catch up to and then zoom
right through. The cold water on my face slaps me. I am
awake and alive; there is nothing but this moment.

DAY 262

Big storm. Watching a storm here is like being allowed to
witness a small God tantrum. You do not want to draw
any attention to yourself. Since we're surrounded by windows, the power of what's happening is undeniable, and
it permeates our beings to the bone. There are no covers
to hide beneath for the shaking of the floor.

The spray from each thundering wave is blown to bits
and then inland, much of it reaching as far as our house.
The whole structure trembles and shudders. We're all
three on the big bed and the dogs are standing on the
floor, front legs on the bed with their heads reaching in,
trying to be with us.

Some spots are more spectacular to watch than others.
We can see one group of rocks that present a vertical cliff
face to the swells. As each wave reaches the rocks it is already toppling over. The booming concussion sounds almost like a gunshot. The wave is always thrust directly
skyward, perhaps a hundred feet, into magnificent walls
of spray.

I love how we just give in—we're not going anywhere.

That is my favorite part, where my important plans are all nullified by the wind. What an excellent thing to have to admit, that a storm is in control of your life!

Our rain barrels fill up and the windmill charges all the batteries.

This storm is bigger than any we have seen. The beaches are rearranged. A slice of a peninsula vanishes; a chunk of rock the size of a school bus, gone. New things wash up: lumber, a dead seal, dead birds, tires, trees, plastic junk, rope, buoys, an oar, a glove, buckets, a doll. Older stuff gets carried off or shifted. Wash-up Point is completely clean. Since we walk around the island several times a week, we notice and appreciate these changes. All our shelves and much of the house is driftwood. Our kitchen counter is the side of a boat that wrecked here years ago.

The storm continues. Ten shingles are blown off our roof. A whole section of earth and trees is removed from the west-facing side of the island. We later find out that one of Peter's sheds washed away. Mike's dock is gone.

For two days we watch the waves. There is nothing between us and Africa but big blue ocean, so the storms have plenty of breathing room, and on this island they exhale. We watch for hours as they tumble toward us, sending spray hundreds of feet inland. The whole island rumbles, and we can feel the vibrations in our bones, a good place to feel anything, one of those places you need to listen to, pay attention to. The waves come here to die, and they are most alive in their dying.

DAY 266

The air smells different today, almost sexy, and I sense stuff underground bubbling with excitement. I feel like a prehistoric hairy guy scratching himself. It is not like it has blown in from somewhere—more like it's bubbled up from the forest, the pregnant earth.

We'll still have some storms—from the east—and maybe will be stranded for two or three days as big seas make the harbor unsafe, but that is it. I think yesterday's snowstorm was the last. The earth has spun itself warmer. It will soon become foggy; half of April and most of May are solid fog. It'll be lobster season then, and there will be maybe five boats with their territories overlapping this is-land. We'll wave, they'll stop by to talk, drink, give us some lobsters, or even break down. I almost like that because I may have a washer or something we can jury-rig for them, and I'll get to be a hero. Having the right part for a guy's engine is the ultimate bonding thing possible out here.

SOMETIMES WHEN WENDY and I fight, it's as if the Terminator has got hold of my soul, of the part of me that wants life to be good, to have things work. I'm steeled. Being right becomes worth dying for, hurling my-self on the sword for. I don't even know what this latest fight is about—something dumb, no doubt. I just hate the ridiculous inevitable escalation. I generally walk away before bad things are said because I really love her.

I sleep alone at the shack and make very small circles in my thoughts. I'm like a ship with no sea room tacking back and forth in the night, unable to see where it is better to be, where I should go to get out. Tacking again and again, imagining shoals in all directions, knowing only that "right here" there is enough water; but even that fades as the tacks get shorter, until all I can do is anchor.

I struggle with myself to have *empathy*. I even look the word up in the *O.E.D.*: "The power of projecting one's personality into (and so fully comprehending) the object of contemplation." And I have that. I'm even good at it. I love my therapist job because I can soul-surf, catch the wave of another's perceptions and feel their balance, catch a view of their horizon. . . . If, however, there is the slightest possibility that my empathy will reveal *how I am* from another's viewpoint, that I am possibly wrong, a jerk, full of shit, etc., then *bammo!* I hit the pier.

Wendy has left all she knows to live in my dream and neurosis. She is demonstrating a level of commitment to me that is frightening.

Could I do that for her? I've given up chasing the opposite sex, something I miss very much. I've given up a certain amount of irresponsibility—something I also miss. There is still a lot more to her than my self-centered universe will ever allow me to understand. She shows me doors where I thought there were only walls.

DAY 267
I had one of my best temper tantrums today and realized a great personal truth: as a bachelor, convinced that the world will end and that I can be saved because I have all

the right equipment, life was much easier than it is now with a family. Most of the stuff I see as essential for survival fits in a fanny pack. My next essential-stuff kit is a backpack. Then my truck, then my sailboat. Each has only the highest-quality items. The fanny pack has the best rope, needles, fire-starting gear, compass, flashlight, first-aid kit, and so on. The backpack has the best one-man tent, sleeping bag, poncho, waterproof clothing, cooking gear, and so on. The truck has the best off-road drive train and half the items needed to establish an entire economy. The sailboat is a perfect refinement of all these.

Anyway, now that I'm with my family I have a much bigger problem, which is this: I've not been able to convince them that the world is ending, so there is a certain urgency lacking in their whole attitude. I buy Stephan a two-hundred-candle-power, waterproof (to six hundred feet), rubber-coated, titanium-framed flashlight, and he carves a Z on the lens with a knife.

So my tantrum: Stephan was dangling the portable CD player by the cord. I realized the pain I felt seeing this valuable thing on the path to its inevitable (in the hands of a now twelve-year-old) destruction. I knew it would eventually be destroyed, but I could not handle the stress of having to wait.

"Everything you touch you break! You're like the god-damn Antichrist of inanimate objects!" I grabbed the CD player and threw it on the ground, obliterating my anxiety.

As these words tumbled from my mouth, and the lid to the player bounced down the stairs, I was thinking that I never am like this; I never destroy things. For a moment I feared that I was unfairly comparing Stephan to myself, then I realized . . . I used to destroy everything too! Things flew apart in my hands, I was entropy incarnate. So how could I be so angry with him?

Am I my father now? Why would I expect a twelve-year-old to be anything but a twelve-year-old? Am I just a spoiled brat wanting to make sure Stephan won't be happy if I can't be happy? How is it possible that I can be so mean?

Perhaps this anger in me bubbles up toward Stephan simply because it can. Maybe I was unable to be angry at my father, and Stephan has his anger . . . so this is what shrinks call "transference"?

All this thinking, and where's the light bulb for me? Where's the release, the end of the movie, where the music swells, Stephan and I desperately running together to embrace? What good is all this "knowing"?

And then, as usual, Stephan wasn't manipulative enough to see anywhere to hide in this conversation, so he said, "I'm sorry, and I'll try to be more careful."

"It's just— Oh shit, I'm sorry too, Stephan. I destroyed everything near me when I was twelve. I'm sorry I'm so mean sometimes, I love you so much . . ."

That was what I meant to say, what I knew was right to say. But it wasn't what I said.

The only word I could speak was "Okay."

Wendy
What a day yesterday. We all fought.
I think we need to get off this island.

15. On My Own

We are conscious of an animal in us, which awakens
in proportion as our higher nature slumbers.

—THOREAU

DAY 277—APRIL

Bright, sunny, and cold morning with pancakes. Wendy
and Stephan are packing for a two-week visit to family in
Idaho. The tension has been building and we all need a
break, me especially. Wendy suggested it as an alternative
to murder or suicide. I agreed.

Just having the plane reservations seemed to calm
things down.

We are all quiet as we ride ashore. We hug. Right before they get into Wendy's car I take a big breath and say,
"Stephan, I love you. I am sorry that I can be such an
asshole."

He smiles. "Ya, you sure can be. I love you too." Then
they are off to a hotel in Halifax so they can get their
early flight tomorrow morning.

Is the only thing that works in my evil-stepfather relationship with this kid *his* ability to love me uncondi-
tionally?

Uncomfortable with the emotions swimming in my stomach, desperate for a distraction, I look around for someone to yarn with. I have always disliked being alone when I say good-byes. I walk toward the water.

The boat is resting on the gravel beach where the tide has left her. The six-foot tides here do not simply flow up and down like the hands of a watch. All tides—as I understand it—move with small jumps, unchanging for a period of time and then dropping or rising quite suddenly. You can see it. So although I left the boat only fifteen minutes ago, the tide has fallen a whole foot. Four hundred pounds of boat and motor are high and dry.

I begin by spinning her around, figuring that she'll be easier to push into the water nose first. When I drag her in stern first I have to lift her over any rock, and the stern is both the boat's heaviest and its least streamlined part. She pivots easily, and I get her around and I push. She makes a small lurch ahead. Suddenly I hear, "*What the hell are you doing?*"

It's Junior, and he appears to be angry.

"Well, uh, I was . . ."

"*Not bow first. You never launch bow first, it's not done, it's just not done!*"

"But she's practically—"

"*I'll not have it.*"

And sure enough, he won't. Made of a combination of tree root and granite, Junior spins my boat around with one gnarled hand so she's stern first to the water. Easy as you like, he shoves her in and hands me the bow line. I'm not sure for what, but I thank him. A little confused, I

pull-start the engine and am off. Peter tosses me a pound
of scallops as I motor past him and Aaron; they are out
dragging.

Later, Aaron explains to me why Junior was so em-
phatic. "Well, yes, you never launch bow first. I watched
a guy do that a couple of seasons ago and he's dead now,
yes he is, by God. You don't mess with the old-timers'
sayings, not here. That'ud be downright stupid. If my
granddaddy heard you say P-I-G on a boat, he'd pick you
up and he'd throw you over the side. Same thing with a
hatch cover—you never turn it over and lay it on the
deck. Never start a voyage on a weekend, especially a Friday
—and there's many more."

I say, "It sounds kinda like the way a church works,
with all the rules, the symbols, the rituals." He replies,
"Well, I don't go to any church so I wouldn't know, but
this is where I live." He gestures to the ocean and the harbor. "And I respect it. This can kill you on a nice summer's
day, and I'm out almost every day. I'll take no chances like
that. I'd rather drive my boat blind drunk to your island
in a gale than say P-I-G on a boat, yes I would . . ."

DAY 278

Rainy noisy night. The water tanks are full and tasting a
little of sulfur. The dogs are depressed. They sleep with
me and then go down to the harbor for their daily activity of waiting. Bear is gone all day, Abby back around
noon looking a little frayed. A good walk around the island. Then I get to thinking:

Wendy requires that I manage the moment. If a seal appears before the house and she doesn't see it, she'll stand there with the binoculars telling me, "Make it come back." This is how she manages the moment, by telling me to do it. This reminds me of an enlightenment course I took in the eighties. In a relationship there are three things a woman wants from a man: *fun* (men are spontaneous and more fun), safety in the *moment* (protection, changing a flat tire, ordering at the restaurant), and *sex*. Males require a *safe place to communicate* (things that they are not comfortable telling men), the *game* of sex and love (the challenge, the "Will I get it?"), and *safety in the future* (the sense that "it will work out"). Providing Wendy with her three things goes a long way.

DAY 281

I sit here missing Wendy, afraid to make the coffee because just two years of her has taught me to be helpless. I miss Stephan. I find myself daydreaming about rowing with him in the harbor, or carrying food up the trail with him and laughing as we trip and stumble. I keep the dogs on the bed with me and we take turns eating spaghetti out of a big pot. They go right for the meatballs.

But I'm also having the best time! Eating Pringles and rum for lunch, mustard and olives for dinner. I love not having my mood changed by someone else's. I can soak in a funk, pee in the sink, eat on the floor with the dogs. . . . It's not that I can't do all these things with my family, but I'm not self-conscious now. "Is this good role-model behavior for my son?" or "I know that grosses Wendy out"—it's just, well, politeness really. I do so many things to be able to live with other humans, to get along, *but I just love to savage out.*

Bonuses of living alone: 1) looking at—well, trying to look at—your butt in a mirror; 2) eating cold baked beans out of the can; 3) reading and reading a good book; 4) dozing; 5) sweeping things into the cracks in the floor; 6) leaving out a dirty magazine (perhaps exposed to sunlight for the first time); 7) sneaking up on the sleeping dogs and blowing in their noses till they wake up; 8) tripling the amount of ground coffee for each pot; 9) barking, howling; and 10) perfecting the really-big-slice theory of eating bread—where you just butter an area of the loaf and go.

So these are the things my soul craves? This is liberation? What have I become?

I have a scallop-dragging day planned—fun to hang with Peter and find our common denominator, where we share roots, so we can talk. I say *fuck* a lot. I'll take a bunch of rum and go to Peter's camp when this southeast wind is gone. I'm taking advantage of being alone and doing big mess-up-the-whole-house repair jobs, like fiberglassing the inside of the whalebone sink. The bone has been drying and a crack has been spreading.

DAY 285

As a rule, I do not give any day the power to be a good or a bad day. To think the *day*, or *God*, or the *CIA*, or any other deity has me on their calendar just doesn't mean anything to me. This being said, however, today was *really a bad day*. I'm toodling along in the boat, having a nice ride in to get mail. I'm thinking about how I've done well this lifetime with lots of near-death experiences, all to the benefit of my appreciating life more, and how it would sure suck to miss the last lesson—that when I do die, it will be alone. The tide is extra high and as usual I'm loving it because everything is changed—all the ledge islands are smaller and I can go over some of the shoals I generally detour around. Unfortunately, I am appreciating this one particular shortcut when a larger than usual swell passes under me. Dead ahead, in the trough of this wave, appears a pointed rock, unquestionably attached to the sea's bottom. The wonderful feeling of floating over the ocean is shattered. I immediately hit the rock with a loud *boom*. The box of emergency gear and I slam ungracefully into the forward seat. An empty oil jug flies past my ear. The next wave picks the boat up and carries us over. Directly in front of me I can see a tear in the bow where the water's rushing in. I stumble back to the stern now, hearing water coming in. Quickly restarting the engine, I accelerate to full throttle, and the bow rises up as we plane over the water. I hurry back to the island and, going fast, drive her a quarter of the way up the ramp before turning the motor off.

The image of the rock rearing its head like that will stay with me. But worse than a fearful picture is the feeling that the ocean seemed to betray me, leaving a hole in the water right before me.

I trust the ocean—it does not have malice—but right now I'm anxious. This uneasy feeling says the ocean did something to me, and I don't like that. The ocean has always been my ally, and I would rather be hunted by an imagined bogeyman than the sea.

I repair the bow using a mallet and the best caulking material I have ever known, 3M's 5200. Those who know the stuff affectionately call it "Fifty-two Million" or even "Fifty-two Billion." I have found few products that live up to their promises. But I don't care, because the label on 5200 makes up for all of them; it is humble: "marine adhesive." Ha! You could join two planets together with this stuff.

Banged roughly into shape, the aluminum bow looks okay—a little wrinkled, as if it aged quickly in just that spot. I drill some holes along the twelve inches of the tear and use stainless steel wire to join them. Then a liberal dose of 5200 to fill up the gaps and cover over all the wire, inside and out. The final touch is several layers of what the inexperienced eye would call duct tape. In 1982 I got a case of this stuff, which calls itself "gaffer's tape, 2-inch black matte." It is usually used in the theater for all the "building" that a stage manager has to do. I use it for anything, including to repair tears in my blue jeans. It will survive about five visits to the washing machine. With the adhesive benefits of the 5200 it is covering, I expect it to last indefinitely.

My boat is repaired. I have to wait two days for the 5200 to dry. To try to cheer myself up I paint the little green boat. I love painting, but I never have the patience to do that brush-dipping thing. With the boat flipped over, I pour half the can on either side of the center line and just push it globbily around. It goos down the edges and I must hurry to spread it before it reaches the rails. I mop the paint along, letting it fill holes here and there. It's a pretty green, and I do feel better. But then it starts raining, and in despair I just walk away, leave my brush on a rock. I want to cry.

DAY 286

Woke to all sorts of birdsong, the guys scratching out territories not so different from humans in their tinted-window bass-thumping small-wheeled cars driving the main drag of a town.

Peanut-butter egg 'n' cheese omelette for breakfast. I lie in bed missing my Wendy, wanting a nuzzle, to hear her laugh.

I count my miseries: 1) a bashed pinkie from hammering the aluminum boat back into shape; 2) an immobile wrist from shucking scallops; 3) a painful other wrist from an old tae kwon do injury; 4) a bruised shin from the boat crash; 5) a twisted ankle from a fall walking around the island yesterday; 6) I'm getting balder by the moment; and 7) I'm still unsure of what to do when I grow up, not to mention when we leave Whale Island.

The dogs still spend most of their day at the dock, waiting for Wendy to return. This is one of those gaps in languages that I just don't like. I have explained it verbally, also believing dogs can read us, and I sent them some vivid mental images. I think they don't perceive the concept of future. I am in good company. They sit and wait patiently. I must admit I love it when I motor into the harbor and they are waiting for me. I'm usually yelling at Abby as I come in—she's either jumping, standing, or swimming right where the boat must go. I believe her brain is so overloaded with the joy of seeing me that the "don't get crushed" instinct is completely inoperative. She lacks peripheral perception.

I love to go walking with them. Abby still stops to eat the rotting sea urchins. Although they are all spines, she has no trouble eating them, or throwing them up. Hell, she can throw up feathers! The duck washed up in November makes frequent cameo appearances now, what with having been torn into at least eleven pieces and the snow melting. It heaves out of Abby in a warmth of fluffy piles.

The paint-and-water mixture I applied to the bottom of the rowboat yesterday has dried nicely. The eventual evaporation of all the water drops has left many depressions on the surface, which will no doubt act like an emergency brake when I'm rowing. Safety first!

DAY 287

As I lock up the house to go ashore I think about territory, and how nice it must be to secure your territory by simply peeing on some of the bigger bushes or trees that surround it.

Visiting in summers is a slow way to establish yourself in the area, and for years small things were stolen from the island. One year, after we'd built most of the main house, a lot was stolen ("By them sons of bitches thievin' goddamn alcoholic Weed Harbor boys," I was told), and I understand it. This is their backyard, and I'm "a rich New Yorker." (Every one from the States is guilty of this unless proven otherwise.) What made me furious was that my "insurance" company would not cover it. I had locked nothing, because these guys could easily get in anywhere, and a big lock might only encourage them to use a chain saw instead of a crowbar. Also, on an island like this, being so remote, a shipwrecked person would be awfully grateful for shelter. It is an unwritten law by the sea, as in any remote settings, that your home is available for shelter. The "insurance" company said that since there was no sign of forced entry, it wasn't really theft. I just about pulled out the rest of my hair when they told me this.

So we keep a seventy-five-cent lock on the door, easily removable. But by now we are safe just because of our presence. Living here makes us human. Besides, this area is too small to steal from quietly. We know who stole from us before, but to take it back or call the police would probably end up with the house getting burned down.

DAY 288
A forty-foot male sperm whale, dead for weeks but still quite whole, has washed into a small cove. Naturally (as

a consumer) my first thought is, "What can I get?" I think of the teeth and scrimshaw, but Peter has already cut the jaws off with a chain saw. He'll get good money for that on some black market. I'll have to wait at least a year for the rest of the bones, which I'll use for building, or sculptures . . . and then I think of the *penis*.

Though I've never heard of an actual penis bone, I have a picture of a sperm whale skeleton that definitely shows a bone down there. Well, wouldn't that be a cool thing to have? What a mantelpiece ornament; imagine the small talk it would elicit.

But I'm afraid to go get it, scared of two things. First, the job itself would be quite gross. I'd wait till low tide and then, with my machete, I'd start hacking away at three and a half feet of penis. Chunks of blubber would be flying, and no matter how hard I tried to stay clean, eventually the whole island would stink.

Second, what if this wakes up the whale? Sure, it's dead, been dead for a month, but if anything can wake up a dead whale, this would be it. It's the look that he would give me that scares me. *His penis is all that he has left.* At one time this guy could hold his breath for an hour and a quarter, dive into the depths of the sea and battle giant squid, sink the *Pequod*. I mean, I'm talking about attempting to castrate Moby Dick!

But the thought of the prize drives me on. The great white hunter, the American male, conqueror of the West. Fearless. I go to the whale with my machete and firm resolve. I take a deep breath of courage. I kick the monstrous penis defiantly. It wiggles, and I run away.

(Weeks later, when Wendy finally sees it, she says, "Holy shit, that's the second-biggest penis I've ever seen!" And I will always love her for saying that.)

DAY 294

Wendy and Stephan are landing in Halifax at eleven-thirty tonight, and I am bubbling with anticipation. Time and distance are the perfect elixir for me, the snake oil that really does work. My relationships are cleaner, more meaningful. I forget bad stuff and I notice the better qualities in others. I listen.

For two weeks I've been a bachelor. And yet, without a doubt, I want my Wendy and Stephan back.

DAY 295

House-shaking windy-ass night with water leaking on the computer, the bed, into a bag of flour. I'm hoping Wendy won't rush to the dock, that the north wind has time to blow some of these big southeast seas flat. I do a high-speed power cleanup: throw rugs down over the dirt, toss a few hopelessly dirty dishes in the woods to "find" again in a few years.

Now it's hailing, blowing thirty knots. But I want my family back real bad, so I will take the boat ashore. It's very gray, penetratingly so, as if the gray were a verb that could sneak under my rain gear, through the seams at my wrists and neck.

One advantage that I have had all year is that Wendy and Stephan really know little about what constitutes bad weather on the ocean. Generally, when I seem confidant, they assume all is well. But truthfully, we have been on this sea in some frightening conditions. I'm pretty comfortable in small boats. I worry that in the future Stephan may feel a bit more invincible than his skill merits.

Hellion of a rough ride in! I can see Wendy's car as I approach the dock; the doors open, and there is my family.

Wendy and Stephan bundle up, jump down into the boat, and we're off for home. They are so excited that any fear they do experience turns to exhilaration.

At our harbor's mouth Wendy is crying happily. Stephan is grinning gleefully, and the dogs are frothing with joy. I feel like a finally found and inserted puzzle piece—we're a family again.

16. Ships at Sea

A single gentle rain makes the grass many sheets greener. So our prospects brighten on the influx of better thoughts. We should be blessed if we lived in the present always, and took advantage of every accident that befell us, like the grass which confesses the influence of the slightest dew that falls on it; and did not spend our time in atoning for the neglect of past opportunities, which we call doing our duty. We loiter in winter while it is already spring.

— THOREAU

DAY 299

Today is the best day of the year as lobster season begins. Last year we were still in Idaho on Setting Day, and we missed all the excitement.

For two months these guys will get up at four A.M. and by maybe two in the afternoon will have pulled, emptied, rebaited, and reset their 250 traps. They will be on the water every day. By sunset I will be able to see hundreds of traps around the island and will have waved and spoken to maybe five guys. We'll be getting occasional meals

—people like to give; there's a good sense of "richness" in passing on a lobster dinner. It is expensive ashore, abstract, while here its value lies in the labor, which is so much more authentic.

I hope the waters have warmed enough; lobsters are like flies and don't move much in the cold.

One guy, who is setting traps in front of my house now, has been doing this his whole life. His dad's nearby in his own old boat, and for three more generations back his family has worked just this five-mile strip of coast. They used to row and sail it, which is why there are all these camps on the mainland shore. The long row back to town was too far, a waste of energy to do every day. There used to be a "canning factory" house out here— two miles west of Whale Island—where the guys could bring their catch and sell it daily. I once found an old chart that showed a footpath leaving Kingsland and heading this way. I looked, but I could never find the path. Aaron's grandfather owns the place still, and there is a sign over the old shed's doorway stating OND BY COOPER; it was put up by Aaron's grandfather's dad. There is a beautiful, deep, and safe cove there, one I'd use in a hurricane. It is between Junior's dock and my island, and I often stop to float quietly in it. I never feel alone when I am there.

After ten months of quiet, the radio and sea are crowded. I can see three boats, and I leave on the VHF all day, listening to the colorful chatter: complaining about the "fucking cold," hopelessness of the catch so far, the calling up of wives at home to order parts, arranging to have a gas truck meet them at the dock, a wife asking for a lobster for dinner, one guy cynically saying, "Ya, I can't keep up with 'um, they're crawling all over the boat, chewin' on me boots." (It is rare to hear a local say he is doing well; "Not too bad" is about as good as you will hear.)

Quiet beauty all over. I am rejoicing at how thin my walls are right now. In my other life I'm not able to leave my heart out front enough, "wear it on my sleeve," but here I can't help it. It strikes me that this is how humans ought to be, that I am experiencing merely what it is to be a human in a natural state of being. I think if I were suddenly deposited in New York City I would become lost like a tear in the rain.

DAY 301—MAY

Stephan begins to massacre the kitchen, making, besides a massacre, what he is calling French toast. His unique style involves frequently putting his hands in his pockets —a look designed, I think, to impress us with how casual an activity this is for him: drop an egg on the floor, put hands in pockets while saying, "Oops!" Pour half a cup of cinnamon into a bowl, say, "Oh no," and put hands in pockets. Melt the spatula, hands go in the pockets. Slip on the egg on the floor, knock over the bowl and the last bit of milk, then put hands in pockets.

At first Wendy and I are edgy, offering suggestions, making sympathetic noises, and secretly relieved that we are on a deserted island in the middle of nowhere. Is this our son, the fruit of our labors, our hope for tomorrow? (A hint for kids: Next time a parent criticizes you, say "Hey, I'm the fruit of your loins, leave me alone!")

After a hurt look crosses his face, Stephan grins and then immediately starts sneezing from inhaling the half cup of cinnamon, which somehow landed on his chest. We just give up the entire parent thing and begin to laugh, to howl with joy. Abby begins licking the cinnamon, and then she sneezes. The spatula bursts into flames. Soon all of us are paralyzed on the floor and clutching our bellies, tears streaming down our faces. I manage to reach the spatula just before the spice shelf catches fire. I throw it out the porch door.

We have cold cereal without milk for breakfast.

DAY 302

Invisible ships at sea blew their Goliath foghorns at one another last night. The deep sound is more felt than heard—a rumble you expect would cause ripples in your hot chocolate. Even with all its fancy radar, a ship may still not see a fishing boat. The horn simply means *Mmmmoooooooooooooooooooovvvvve.*

By morning it is still foggy, but also bright. We can hear the local boats working their traps. From his camp north of Whale Island, Percy's *Heavenly Girl* appears, Jarvis barking on her bow, and in a moment they are gone.

Day 306

Beautiful clear north-wind morning, still cold. Colorful boats and lobster pots everywhere, the season is on! Between clouds Stephan types a report, using solar power to run the laptop. Peter calls on the VHF and invites us all for lobster at his camp. "When Stephan finishes his report," I tell him. The keys immediately start clicking away at twice the speed they had been. I had no idea Stephan could type. He's so excited that clouds seem to scurry out of the sun's path, the solar panels drinking deeply.

Stephan likes Peter, loves to be around him. They don't really talk that much. I think Stephan just likes being with another man. He and I can be so locked into fixed patterns with each other, automatic, predictable. I think he feels heard by Peter, and I know Peter enjoys the company. Stephan listens to Peter's words as if they are the best bits of bait in Nova Scotia.

DAY 307

This whole year seems a love story. Wendy and I go to bed as early as we can and just snuggle, lying nose to nose, and it's been so wonderful, so rich, like sleeping on a mattress-sized slice of warm rye bread, sinking in with wisps of steam floating by, and pulling another warm slice over you for a blanket. We huddle down till the sun's well up, till we can't even pretend it's not lunchtime . . . and the day goes along with brief hand-holding, rubs, and glances. Wendy likes nothing better than a steamy fondle while she's making bread. Her head arches back just a little.

The intensity of this happiness obliterates the memory of past hardships. What value is there in listening to what those gargoyles who wait at the doors of perception are yelling in their contorted voices? Should our lives be spent wrestling, and thus becoming these demons? I think not. I prefer to expose them to intense bursts of joy. Who's to say which is real? I'd rather live with my illusions.

DAY 308

Swallows, yellow-rumped warblers. A big female hairy woodpecker lets us get within about fifteen feet of her on the trail. It is spring on our island, and around here, that means *fog!* I'm stuttering to describe it, to convey all the emotions it elicits. It can be so thick and enfolding, and when you are boating in it, strange urges take you over, saying, "No, go *this* way, the compass must be wrong," and when you think you're going straight, in just a quarter mile—five city blocks—you can make a complete circle, crossing your own wake. Rocks, trees, buoys, boats, birds, shallows, waves, and any number of objects you can hallucinate—all these things can suddenly loom up before you. Uncertainly, you stare—which is a mistake—at some shape. It vanishes, then closer something else appears. And when you're really lost, maybe an island appears where it can't possibly be, and your mind is trying to explain what force put it there, *moved it there,* rather than comprehending that you are utterly lost.

I've heard screen doors slamming and a "Here, kitty kitty" when I was sure I was miles offshore. I have heard a woman's throaty laughter just feet away. Once an angel appeared, her wings spreading, stretching, and then she vanished, lightly pulled apart by wind, and I suddenly saw a big ugly rock with surf over it just where she floated.

I have wandered like a billiard ball careening off imaginations gone wild. One big uncontrolled therapy session.

DAY 310

The woodpecker visits on the roof, tap tap tapping, doing some drilling too, but then she gives up and is gone for grubbier pastures.

Sometimes I worry: What will I have to panic about tomorrow? I handle transition by being only a day or two ahead, but it is spring now, and that definitely means that summer is next. We will have to leave here then.

We're about out of money—just enough to get back to Idaho and pay a few months' rent. We need jobs. Though Stephan wants to stay here forever, I think Wendy is beginning to feel like a prisoner. I try to ease this with trips ashore, and I give her lots of chocolate, but it's not enough. There is a limit to how self-centered I can be. I don't mean to imply that I am not way past most people's limit —I know that I am. But this is my Wendy, my love, the woman I want to grow old with. She isn't happy here.

Still, I am avoiding making plans. I am a little kid with his fingers in his ears yelling the national anthem in an attempt to drown out any unfamiliar thoughts.

We've no jobs in Idaho, no place to return to, but Wendy already knows her dog-walking route. I'm stretching my ability to think ahead, wondering if using acetone on the windowsills will help the new caulking stick better. I'm very happy with this scope of responsibility, essentially that of a child defending a sand wall on the beach from the incoming tide, as noble a cause as any.

Wendy eagerly balances our checkbook. All those little numbers have been getting smaller. I think she is happy with that; it is an inarguable reason for us to have to return to Idaho.

That night I dream. Wendy is a great big plant that has been pulled out of the ground. Her roots are wiggling in the air and looking for nourishment. Stephan comes upstairs from his room; he wants to play cards. He too is a plant, also rootless, with small clods of dirt falling about him.

Each branch of their roots become smaller, eventually ending as a small root hair. I can see that each of these are hungry, wiggling in search of water and minerals. I run to the sink and begin filling a bucket with water. I pour in a whole bowl of sugar, some leftover bread, and an apple. I look around the room in a panic: What else can I add? In a frenzy I pore over my precious bookshelves and choose a field guide to butterflies, an abridged encyclopedia, and *Still Life with Woodpecker*, by Tom Robbins. I throw in a Chopin CD, a flashlight, a candle, and a pair of wool socks.

I bring my bucket to my family, but it is too late. Their leaves are drying, withering before me.

I wake up.

17. A Place I Never Meant to Leave

Only in silence and solitude can you find your true self.

—A YOGI I SAT NEXT TO
AT A MOVIE THEATER IN 1976

DAY 311

I want to stay forever. I want to become a professional scrounger, find a way to make seaweed taste good, trade labor for outboard-engine gas—better yet, trade the boat in for an old sailboat. Something small, flat-bottomed, easy for one person to operate. Grow potatoes, set out fish traps, hunt, grow a beard, forget my social security number.

Stephan will become a child of the forest, moving silently through the brush and catching animals with his bare hands. With one of those *Russian Women Seeking American Husbands* catalogs we will get him a wife raised barefoot in the Siberian tundra. We will build them a log house in the darkest center of the island. He can raise wolves! And Wendy could—

With a screeching halt my fantasy comes to an end.

DAY 312

Two days ago I watched something odd float by. It was sort of yellow, looked to be maybe four feet by six feet, and it was conforming to the ocean's surface, shaping itself into waves, like a big paint spot, or a sheet of cardboard maybe. I watched it through binoculars—it was just that sort of day, I guess—and then it drifted out of sight behind some rocks.

The next day Wendy and I were walking around the island, stopping every so often to smooch . . . and there, laid out on the rocks before us, was the mattress last seen on Day 196 skipping over the trees. *It's back!*

We continued our walk around the island and almost had sex in the moss, but I inhaled a blackfly and while I was hacking, I farted loudly and Wendy seemed to fall out of the mood. Sigh. It's okay, though; I'm sure I'll remember it as having been better.

DAY 314

Gorgeous morning. I'm off to help Peter pull his fishnet. He generally catches schools of mackerel, which appear this time of year. The trap is about a quarter mile of straight net, fifty feet high (from the surface of the ocean to the bottom). Fish hit this wall and follow it into another net, which traps them. There are thirty-six anchors, hundreds of buoys, probably five miles of heavy line, and a drawstring on the bottom of the trap net—I think. Honestly, I haven't been able to figure out how it really works, despite numerous descriptions. Anyway, it's a big

deal to haul it up, so friends show up and each'll get
percent of the catch. If it's empty, the net will take one ᴏ
two hours to haul. Full of fish, half a day.

We meet at Peter's wharf as the sun rises. There ar
eight boats with eight guys waiting to get started. Ther
is a lot of scratching and smoking, and I'm trying to fit in.
Just trying to understand what is being said is difficult for
me, because when in even small local herds, men's lan-
guage can become very dialectal. Even Peter's words are
hard to follow. Suddenly over the VHF radio comes my
wife's voice. On fishing boats the radio is always on. It's
also loud enough for you to hear it over the engines. On
eight boats, over eight speakers, Wendy wants to discuss
what I'll be making for dinner, and she starts off about
pasta and sautéed chicken and, well, my cover is blown:
around here no guy would admit to using the word *sauté*.
The guys cough and pretend not to hear.

The haul is difficult, lots of back and forearm stuff. A
hundred-pound seal has gotten tangled in the net and is
dead. Seals are smart enough to know that a net provides
good fish, but sometimes they get caught and drown.
They can also tear the net and ruin the catch. I remember
in the late 1960s, when I was a feel-good liberal, a real
"save the seals" kind of kid. Now here I am with these
guys, who absolutely hate the things; a single seal can
cause hours of repairs and thousands of dollars in lost
fish, maybe a fifth of a yearly income.

It's a good lesson for me. Most environmental causes
are funded by people like me who want to save the forest

but live in a wood house, buy fish from the store and have SAVE THE SEALS bumper stickers, want to preserve the Alaskan wilderness from oil drilling but drive a climate-controlled luxury vehicle and complain about gas prices. The guys here cut trees for their homes, shoot seals when they can, hunt, and spend their lives far closer to the cycles of our earth than I ever will. Are they better? No. But they are congruous.

More hauling . . . and amazingly, in this whole huge trap, we get a total of two fish, two crabs, the dead seal, and lots of tiny crustaceans, which look like the ocean's version of stick bugs.

DAY 320

Is it just me, or do many men occasionally find themselves in hiding from their families, a refugee?

Right now I'm sitting in the boat, high and dry on the ramp. I've just finished bending the prop back into its general shape, filling the gas tank, restowing the life jackets, drying out the lines, and taking inventory of the survival gear. I am Robinson Crusoe locked in his stockade, clutching his few possessions and peering out for savages.

My fort, this boat, is the only comfort I can find right now. She is a small masterpiece, her readiness and willingness to survive being my best creation.

How like a child I am, at thirty-nine, a guy hiding in his secret fort. I could take her to sea right now, alone. Perhaps this fantasy of escape is what allows me to stay. That and some rum.

Near my head is a small globe of a compass mounted

out of harm's way, under a seat. I've watched its direction for years now, and it always works, always sits on the surface of this earth pointing out where to go. Just beyond it are some courses written in Magic Marker on the inside of the boat. To get from the harbor here on Whale Island to the mouth of Strawberry Passage (passing perfectly between the hazards of Black's Ledge and "The Breaker") I must go 257 degrees. Then 215 degrees to the rocks by Jason Island, 265 degrees into Jason's Channel, and so on, till 355 degrees brings me to Junior's dock. I love my compass. It responds to forces unchanging, unlike my stepson.

Two pieces of plywood cover the fore and aft aluminum floors. They are less slippery than the aluminum and reinforce the hull so that when I drop heavy things, assuming they've missed my toes, they stay in the boat, thus preventing the ocean from coming in.

Next I have a big blue Tupperware bin, two feet by three by one. It sits low and stays closed no matter what. From this box I am equipped to deal with most of what this life throws at me . . . except for the world of people. For that I have the rum. Anyway, the box contains a collapsible fishing rod, a mess of lures and hooks, a fishing reel, a bag of plastic bags (small zipper-locks, garbage-bag size, and one big enough to drive this whole boat into, twenty feet by ten by ten), a collapsible shovel with a saw hidden in the handle, binoculars (adjustable, 8 to 20 power), three plastic adapters for gas-line hose, and a chart of this shoreline (double-laminated). Naturally, there is also a hundred feet of parachute chord.

Next are two packages—the ones to grab if I'm washed ashore, or out to sea, or if I have to establish another consumer-based society on an island, for instance. First is a small bullet- and waterproof black case containing a portable VHF with three battery packs, two 20,000-candlepower flashlights with two spare battery packs, one spare bulb, two spare spark plugs, and some copper "paint," which conducts electricity. The next grab is my favorite. It is a fanny pack, and with it on I feel invincible: four candles, three lighters, and one flint-and-steel fire starter. Hypothermia medicine (Jell-O powder). Pliers, screws, hose clamps, cotter pins, pulley (eight-hundred-pound), and spark-plug wrench. Flare gun with five flares, signal mirror, and a six-by-six-foot neon signal cloth, "the loudest whistle on earth." (It also works underwater. You never know when you'll need to call Flipper.) One quart of water. A hammer, a twelve-inch screwdriver, a roll of duct tape, an assortment of stainless steel bolts, vise grips, a Phillips-head screwdriver, pliers, one of those plier tools that claims to be a whole tool kit, an eight-inch tube of epoxy, another two of those twenty-by-ten-by-ten-foot garbage bags, two handheld flares, and three ten-inch big-ass motherfucking nails. Also thirty-six hundred calories of compressed Coast Guard–approved "food."

Outside the Tupperware box now are fourteen gallons of fuel, two liters of oil, one liter of "dry gas," a handheld bilge pump, a funnel, a canteen, an extra drain plug, a fifty-foot coil of line, two stainless steel knives easily accessible by reaching under the fore or aft seats, my

25-horsepower outboard, two oars, a spare 3-horsepower engine (stowed forward with three sets of foul-weather gear), a block and pulley, another fifty-foot coil of rope, three life jackets, one army poncho, a twenty-foot bow-line always attached to the boat, and 250 feet of anchor line coiled down in a bucket and ready to feed out, one end already secured to the boat . . . and a bottle of rum. Did I mention that already?

This is a tiny boat, just fifteen feet long, and me, quite drunk by now, and we're ready for any seas, any Cape Horn voyage. (Nietzsche comes to mind: "One can endure to live in a meaningless world because one organizes a small portion of it oneself.") This is bliss for me; it gets no better. Ah wait, it does. Bear is with me. We have been together since he was twelve days old. He likes the plywood decking too, and is asleep in a cuddle knot right now with me, his ear tips trembling with his every heartbeat. When I stand up and grab the outboard for support, he's at the bow, tongue and tail wagging in the wind and eager for whatever adventure we can fall into.

DAY 322

Today it rained just when we were running out of water —we have have made it all year with our own rainwater system and I am filled with pride as if I controlled the weather. Heavier rain as the day goes on. . . . Years ago, when I sailed my small boat for a year using only a sextant for navigation, the same "luck" followed me. I was able to catch enough of a glimpse of the sun on all but three days out of 312, enough sun to work out my position on the globe. What rules these phenomena? Or is it merely interpretations that order it so?

DAY 334—JUNE

We saw a whale! It was maybe forty feet long and swam just two hundred feet from our porch. Its back fin had a bizarre upside-down-zucchini look to it, so I think that it was a common blackfish. As usual I was reaching for my guidebook, and missed its second surfacing.

Stephan finished school today, and I wonder what he has learned. I have regurgitated many a morsel into that gullet—has any of it become the child? I tried to teach him about thinking, not facts. I don't think he learned much from the schoolbooks, and that is okay. Truthfully, they were a distraction. I wanted him to read great literature, for books are good friends. I did not want to taint reading by associating it with school, which already is in the category of "work" for him.

Right now he is engrossed with *Little Big Man*, a terrific book I first read only last week. Other books he has devoured this year include *Huckleberry Finn*, *Tom Sawyer*, *The Brothers K*, all of Vonnegut, lots of science fiction and fantasy, *In the Shadow of Man*, *The Giver*, *The Lust Lizard of Melancholy Cove* and *Practical Demonkeeping* by Chris Moore, *We the Living*, *A Connecticut Yankee in King Arthur's Court*, the whole *Shōgun* series (four books at twelve hundred pages each), the Foundation trilogy, and even several editions of the *World Weekly News*!

(Sometimes feeding the hunger is better than worrying about nutrition.)

And these are just some. He read thirty-two other books.

When I am feeling especially hopeless about being a good dad I think of Stephan's passion for books. Did I "give" him that? Can I take some credit, or do I need to pass it off to the books themselves, the passions of their authors?

I know I encouraged it, and yes, I will take a little credit here. I am proud of him.

Cupcakes are the universally understood reward for completing a year of education. Stephan and Wendy bake up a batch and I retrieve a hidden can of vanilla icing I've been saving for today. Wendy insists it must be properly stirred; then she and Stephan lick the knife clean. Stephan points out that they forgot to spread it on the cupcakes. They do that, then lick the knife clean. Wendy notices there is leftover icing, and spreads more on the cupcakes. Then she and Stephan lick the spoon clean.

DAY 343

The alarm speaks, Wendy and I roll over. It's four-fifteen and the sky's just light enough to show some red. Wendy puts water on to heat; I wake up Stephan.

Yesterday as I passed Peter's fish trap, Stephan and I noticed odd ripples lined up on the surface, and not by the wind. I turned into Peter's small harbor and yelled the news. He didn't believe me, but hell, I'm from New York. I understand.

Warm clothes and two mugs of coffee slammed down. Wendy goes back to sleep and Stephan and I are off in our boat as the sun's drearily rising into the gray. At Peter's wharf we meet up with all the guys. Four boats, eight people.

Grunt, haul, moan, complain, and pull. Stephan pulls as hard as anyone. After half an hour we see swirls and a two-foot-diameter whirlpool begins on the far side of the net. We see green and blue. Mackerel, and lots.

Two hours later and Peter's boat is full. The fish are level with the lower deck rail: two and a half by sixteen by twenty feet of solid fish—twenty-seven thousand pounds. That is six and a quarter cords of spasmodically wiggling fish, like a huge tub of Jell-O giving birth to four hundred thousand worms! Even at today's low market price of seventy-five cents per pound, that's a good haul.

Stephan and I return home triumphantly covered in fish scales. We burst into the house and give Wendy a great big bear hug. She almost wiggles out, but having spent the last three hours with things wiggling and trying to get away, Stephan and I hang on tight. Finally she gives up and laughs with us. Abby begins licking the scales off Stephan.

We all take showers and I fall asleep on the floor listening to a Verdi CD. I can just hear Stephan's headphones downstairs; Queen, I think. The dogs, as if they too fished, collapse on and around me, exhausted. Wendy smiles.

DAY 344

The ants are back. They wander about the house, helping themselves to the food the dogs miss. I don't mind that. But sometimes during a meal it begins raining pieces of insulation and sawdust from the roof, just a drizzle, yet annoying because it's my house and their eating means I have less of my house. So, I sprayed Raid in the cracks on the ceiling. Then it hailed writhing ant bodies for a few days, and that was more annoying, because although ants have a pleasing lemon-drop flavor, these were poisoned. In town I buy a new and improved ant-killer poison. It is a "slow-acting poison" you feed them, which "they bring back to the nest to feed their larvae." Now when I see an ant I run after it and hold the tube upside down, like a baby bottle, and nurse out a drop, and the ant stands up on his hind legs and holds the nipple like a child and sucks in the poison. Then I must watch and follow him back to the nest so that any of the twelve other feet in the house do not on purpose or accidentally kill him. It takes about five minutes per ant, and so far I've lovingly fed and protected maybe seven of them. I neglected one for just a moment on his way home, and I heard a loud stomp and a cry of "Die, you essence of evil!" from my adorable wife. The only unethical part of this, the part I feel bad about, is that I don't have to experience the killing of baby ants. I know I'm doing it, but I am too comfortably safe. I should suffer a little.

Wendy

I want to get back to civilization bad. I have no women to sit and have coffee and talk over my day with, or to complain with and strategize on how I can do better. I miss walking out my door and going for a jog or hiking up the mountains with my dogs. I miss yard-saling.

DAY 347

Stephan says, "Shit," his first out-loud curse ever. Wendy cries. I take him outside for a brief lecture: "Not in front of your mother."

DAY 350

I sat down today and came up with a partial list of what we consumed or produced this year. These things were all imported to our island—except for the wood, the fits, and the water (we made or collected those here).

- peanut butter, 21 lbs.
- coffee, 28 lbs.
- flour, 110 lbs.
- onions, 80 lbs. of white, 140 lbs. of red
- toilet paper, 0.2 miles
- baked beans, 62 cans
- corn, 88 cans
- water, 2,000 gallons
- ketchup, 4 gallons
- Parmesan cheese, 18 lbs.
- cabbage, 30 heads
- soy sauce, 4 gallons
- beer, 96 bottles; 2 bottles of gin, 3 of vodka, 5 of tequila, and 12 of rum
- chocolates, 12 lbs.
- wood, 4.9 cords
- dog food, 600 lbs.
- laundry, 3.5 cords
- propane, 380 lbs. total (1.04 lbs. daily)

−duct tape, between 300 and 400 feet
−dust, approximately three big garbage bags worth
  generated: 60% dog hair, 20% sawdust, 5% scraps
  of food, 5% body detritus, 9% parts of things that
  went *boink* or *tinkle* when I tried taking them apart,
  1% disintegrated house from the ants
−ammunition, 120 12-gauge shells (two ducks killed)
−.30-30 rounds, about 100 (no kills but several broken rocks)
−paper towels, 0.4 miles
−Prozac, 0.6 lbs.
−aspirin, 2.2 lbs.
−Q-Tips, 400
−kerosene, 20 gallons
− 1-inch-diameter candles, 250 feet
−socks: worn out, 22 pairs; lost to Abby, 23 pairs
  (maybe sprouting in the woods by now)
−Monopoly, 47 games played
−electricity: in one year we used the equivalent of one
  electric stove with its broiler and all four burners
  going for one hour
−outboard-engine gas, 150 gallons
−tar, 10 gallons
−assorted glue, 4 lbs.

Major fits:
I'm leaving. (4)
I'm dying. (7)
You make my life hell. (16)

What the hell am I doing here? (15)

I have no life. (44)

We're out of chocolate! (1) (And it was so awful I will be sure never to let it happen again.)

DAY 355

Today is cleaning day. Wendy is up at five A.M. In pathetic protest I lie in bed till an ammonia stink lifts me awake. I hide under the table, pretty well sheltered from her storm. Rags fly about; dust has no chance to settle.

My favorite cleaning technique can be done only on windy days. With doors closed I sweep frantically for five minutes, starting up high and working down. The idea is to stir up all the dirt. When the air reaches its saturation point, I quickly open all the doors and windows, and everything is sucked or blown out (the distinction depends on which door you open last). Needless to say, this is not Wendy's preferred cleaning technique; I am sent to the porch, and just in time to have a rug beat on me. I climb down onto the dirt and the window-washing water (vinegar, ammonia, and soap) hits me in the back.

Then, with a squeaky-clean home and therefore ready for Judgment Day, we saunter around the island in our underwear.

Ducks! The eiders have released their babies, and sometimes two or three families will team up. Bald eagles are their number one enemy. We see six parents and twenty-two ducklets together right now. The little ones try to dive, disappearing beneath the surface for only the briefest moment, because they are too buoyant, or their paddle feet are not strong enough yet. Then they boink out, squirted from the sea like pinched watermelon seeds. They look surprised to be on the surface again.

I'm content here, and I'm watching the seasons go by and I want to stay forever this simple. I can hear an outboard, Kingsland's foghorn, the bell buoy off Weed Harbor, a high note of wind in the trees, a distant surf. The house shudders in the wind, small gusts shaking the glass globe in the lamp. A birdsong, another deeper background wind noise, some specific waves.

I could never listen this completely before. I have stood in our harbor and heard water being dragged through seaweed, a jellyfish turning over, a ripple being reflected off a rock. Just for these new sounds in my life I want to stay here forever.

DAY 356

Lobstering with Peter the other day I was struck by something about human nature. There's a small wire cage in each trap that he stuffs with mackerel or whatever he's baiting with that day, but when he catches a live fish he'll use it. What he does is hold it in both hands, then in one strong motion tears it almost in half, folds it, and stuffs it in the cage. There is no flapping— it's as instant a death as you could want, and that is what struck me. I want to die as *firmly for a purpose* as the fish. The hands are experienced and the grip sure, solid, fatherly. There is no joy, no sadness or anger, just motion, purpose, and focus. To die in those hands you would not be alone; you would flow into Peter.

Then I thought of Peter's role out here in this wilderness, his closeness to life and dying, his hands-on participation. He barely finished high school; he rarely reads a book. And yet I would trust myself in his strong hands without pause. In his life there is no need for fax machines or decaf. His life is intertwined with these waters, this piece of Nova Scotia coastline. He's been here his whole life and in those forty years has been as dependable as any tree to grow, lobster to hunt, or duck to fly. He walks between points directly. Yet when he is in his boat you will see him take the longer route, pause to feel the wind blow on his face, catch the sun's reflection on the water, watch the way a wave breaks. He may not be comparing what he sees to something Homer describes; he's experiencing it firsthand. He cannot explain God—he would not try. He is too close. If I were suddenly in Peter's inner world I'd be screaming, "*I'm here, this is it! Oh wow, where is my camera? Quick, a pen, I gotta save this!*" But Peter was never so far away that arriving was a big deal.

One thing I love about Peter is his ineptness ashore. His wife and three daughters, the house, the well, the money, the mortgage, calculating pounds of fish into dollars—he does all these with a shrug. He's tried to master them, can't, knows it, and no longer frets about it. If there was an old Victorian painting of him and his family he would be apart, looking uncomfortable and perhaps gazing downhill, toward his boat. When I've sat in his liv-

ing room, no two minutes have gone by without his looking through binoculars toward the sea.

I will never forget hunting with this man. We separated
to meet at a ravine over a hill. I was immediately lost, and
half an hour later was noisily clinging to the top of a tree,
looking over miles and huge distances of bog and spruce
forest. Then suddenly, just fifty feet away, there was Peter,
his face smiling appearing from a clump of alder. What
struck me was his quiet. Though wearing a bright orange
vest he was invisible to my panicked eye. It was as if he
hadn't walked to meet me there but was at home the
whole time. Only I in my panic perceived the concept of
somewhere else, being lost. Peter lives found.

DAY 358

When I worked as a counselor there was a visualization
process I would do with kids to help them turn negative
memories into positive learnings. I have done it so often
that I was not surprised to wake up this morning having
dreamt this process. I was Stephan's negative memory.

In my dream, something was not right with Stephan.
I had to fix him, as if he were the problem. His image was
projected onto a big and far away movie screen at a
drive-in theater. The image was muddled, unfocused, and
imperfect. The screen slowly inflated into a huge balloon
and began to float up. As I watched, the image on the balloon changed from murky Stephan into me, also muddled
and imperfect. The balloon continued to rise, and suddenly my image clarified into an old an cynical man. I
thought to myself that that old man had nothing to offer,

that he should just keep on floating so that the next generation could enjoy their lives without this old man's baggage to burden them. I started to cry as the balloon floated up, away from me.

Then the balloon popped, exploding into thousands and thousands of tiny parts, which fluttered down toward the earth. As they fell through the clouds, they became snow.

The snow fell toward the earth. Then Stephan was there, and in childlike glee, he raised his hands and jumped as the snow settled around him. He laughed.

Slowly dawn began, dark blue turning to steel blue and then warm blue. The sun appeared. Stephan watched the colors shift as the snow began to melt around him. The ground roiled with growth, and I saw grass and trees climbing upward. Stephan held his arms out, bathing in the luscious morning light. An apple tree grew up before him, its flowers pink, and Stephan reached out to touch it. He was smiling.

I woke up.

DAY 359

Stephan and I are walking and jumping around the island —my favorite and only sport of this year. I like to go from rock to rock building up speed, so that pretty soon there's no thought, just a motion trance of momentum and balance . . . and then I notice that I've been repeating a mantra woven into my bliss: "A sprinkle a day helps keeps the odor away . . ." Oh, wouldn't some advertising executive be overjoyed to know that his "work" is still being sung by a baby boomer twenty years later? Meanwhile Stephan is landing on every other rock with a cry of "Got milk?" What a pair we are.

During breakfast Stephan said he never wanted to leave the island. Wendy said, "But what about your friends in Idaho?" and he replied, "Mom, out here there are no people to have to be with, no large city problems, no civilization. I love it!"

The look Wendy gave me almost caused the toast I was bringing to my mouth to burst into flame. "Hmm, I wonder who he got that from?" she asked. I began to reply something about him being a free thinker, but she cut me off with a "Shut up" and a small grin. I nodded my "Yes, dear."

And I am proud! Real puffy-chest strutting material. I want to call my dad and tell him that *at least something from me* is going to survive for another generation. Doesn't this make me immortal? And just wait until Stephan gets older and can add his own flavor to this! Maybe he *will* live out here with a wild woman and raise wolves.

Now would be a good time to die, I think to myself.

DAY 360

Our walks around the island are becoming sad for me—how can such a wonderful daily event be coming to an end? I feel the heaviness of an awful momentum, an inevitability. We'll have to go back.

DAY 362—JULY

We know many of the rocks by look and feel. Being habitual creatures, we often follow the same route, and it's magic to feel that sharp point, that same slippery place . . . and the boulder that rolls around in the storms. Today we found a live baby duck washed up, threw him back into the sea. I'll miss the adventure of each walk, what to find. I fell once and landed with my face two inches from some beautifully faceted quartz crystals.

DAY 363

Today the house is too small, so Wendy determines that the laundry must be done immediately, and I bring her ashore in stormy seas. We get soaked from waves of green water, roiling spray. We're so wet that Wendy just laughs the last mile. We decide I should write a book called *I Risked My Life for Laundry,* or maybe *Heroes Wear Only Clean Clothes*. It's joyful, riding up and down each wave, flowing around the wavelets on the waves. In some places the bottom shoals quickly, and the seas break suddenly, and we motor past thousands of tons of curling motion. Maybe the book will be called *The Driveway from Hell*.

But what a driveway it is! It separates the civilization from the wilds so clearly. We all should have a moat like Wemmick in *Great Expectations,* a symbolic demarcation between our public and private selves. Telephones violate that with a vengeance.

The biggest seas come in groups of three and are most intense in certain areas. At one point things get scary and Wendy screams. I hate that, because a woman's panic scream at a tense moment like that signifies just one thing—imminent death—and, well, I'm busy steering, and the imminent-death shriek dumps about a quart of adrenaline into my body, and this doesn't help me negotiate the fluidity of the sea, as I've almost broken bones going rigid with *her* fear . . . but the sea doesn't quite break on us, and with a loud "Don't scream at me!" we're off toward the next wave, and Wendy is embarrassed.

As usual, Stephan is riding in the bow. He sits in the middle of the seat, stretching his arms out on either side, holding tightly to the rails. As the boat leaps he lets out joyful cries of "Yahoo!" and "Yippee!"

DAY 365

Clusters of balloons wash up on these shores. Multi-colored wrinkles of rubber sometimes tied with ribbons, sometimes with white string. Sometimes one, sometimes ten. Sometimes all popped, or maybe just very low on helium, half deflated and embarrassingly wrinkled.

A white balloon with a purple ribbon sags before me. It washed up many mornings ago and I hung it up to remind me of all the intense bursts of life going on around me that I miss. If I were psychic I could see an aura around it.

The balloon should not exist. A wish, a dream, it has no place existing to wash onto my beach, unless my beach were of another world. It's like finding all the blown-out-for-a-birthday-wish candles, the lost teddy bears, the single favorite socks.

Maybe my island here is the designated place for balloons to wash up. The waves come here to die too.

Waves are motions that carry energy, but not matter, from one place to another. They pass along their energy as if it were a hot chestnut. When two people are holding a rope tightly between them and one flicks his end, a wave will move down the rope. The person at the other end will feel all the force of the first person but the end he is holding has not changed.

An ocean wave is an edge of water wind has gotten under. Over continent-sized distances at sea the waves grow. In 1998 a one-hundred-foot wave was recorded off North Carolina. That is like the Empire State Building lying on its side and rolling toward you with alacrity. Waves are, like icebergs, bigger beneath the water. Much bigger. They can move sand on the ocean's floor to a depth of 660 feet. But it is not the water from across an ocean that washes up on my shore; it is a restless spirit of the earth.

A wave may travel thousands of miles at up to six hundred miles per hour. A wave's energy can be months old, especially around Cape Horn, the bottom of South America, where they can blow around and around the globe without washing onto any shore.

The wind, with some help from the moon and the earth's rotation, causes the wave. It travels fully expressed for great distances. It playfully licks ships as it passes, lobs sea ducks into the sky, and makes tiny air currents, which albatrosses use to glide on, flying for hours just inches from the sea without a single wing flap.

As the wave approaches the shore its bottom is pushed up, the top reaching higher into the storm, where it is torn by wind, shredded some, but still deeply whole and moving. It builds itself higher and higher, until, unable to support its reach for the sky, it tumbles and roars onto the shore, the hardest substance it has known since its creation. Then, no longer united, each drop of it is flung about, dissipated.

What is so wonderful, what makes each wave a story as deep as a human life, is that it's not the water traveling great distances, just the energy. Are we these bodies, these suits of meat? Each particle of water makes a small circle, receiving and then transferring the wind, moon, and earth's spin onto another drop of water. Is that any different from our own doings in this life?

So there is no body to a wave, only motion. When our tired bodies finally wash ashore, our living energy spent, our loved ones must struggle to separate our bodies from our souls, so that that energy lives on in their memories. Their idea of heaven—of whatever happens to us when our bodies die—that's where we do continue to live, how we become immortal. I have noticed that this is what I strive for so much, not to be gone when I'm dead, my life's mist at least getting another wet.

One of my near death experiences was in a big storm when my dad and I were sailing around Cape Horn. The wave that lifted our small boat to seemingly impossible heights threw us down the front of itself moving too fast for the boat to stay in the water. Falling and then floating in the enormous chaos, I thought, completely and wonderfully helpless, of the power around me, the beautiful force of the sea, and how it was difficult to really appreciate it unless you were in a situation like my own. I felt sadness that I would be unable to share this moment, that I would have to take it with me, alone. I wanted someone who would continue living to know about this particular death. Like Peter, I just wanted to be immortal.

I watch waves here build in the shallows—building as the bottom comes up and tumbles the top till it slams into a cold inarguable rock, bursts into the air with thunderous power. I hear the booming half a mile away. A mass of ocean travels white straight up. The winds slowly pull out the mist and then the pieces till it is all translucent, and all that adventure, all that chaos, that fury, is dissipated in the winds. And I am there to see it.

Yesterday on a walk around the island I heard and felt a wonderful deep grumbling under a small cliff where fairly large seas were expressing their last. On my belly I crawled to the edge and peeking over, I could see a huge green boulder rolling back and forth. It had smoothed a large bowl out of the bedrock—a bowl big enough to sit a family in—and it was thudding this and that way, slowly grinding a hollow in the bedrock, already quite smooth and patient with time.

I watched for many waves and felt its motion relax my body. Deep thudding, when not accompanied by anxiety, is a wonderful penetrating bone message. I am hopeful that my life will be as deliberate as this rock, that I will leave a perfect expression. I want for Stephan to always have me in his heart. I want for him to live fully, to be all used up when he dies. And also for him to pass on a part of his soul, just a little mist, to his own child.

Epilogue

I went to the woods because I wished to live deliberately, to front only the essential facts of life, and see if I could not learn what it had to teach, and not, when I came to die, discover that I had not lived.

I left the woods for as good a reason as I went there. Perhaps it seemed to me that I had several more lives to live, and could not spare any more time for that one. It is remarkable how easily and insensibly we fall into a particular route, and make a beaten track for ourselves.

—THOREAU

SIX MONTHS LATER IN IDAHO

I awake already startled, unsure of at what exactly, but I can feel that it is something alien to the life I perceive as human. There it is again. It's the starting of the number two jet engine of the 7:05 flight to Salt Lake. The airport is directly across the street.

It is the concept of "background" noise that is bothering me. I fly; I know it makes noise—that's not what I mean. It's the *not* hearing, that we can and do learn to close off our awareness and our senses. When I lived in New York City I had to not notice a man sleeping in a doorway. I had to exercise a muscle that I am embarrassed to even have, the "Oh, that's somebody else's problem" muscle. So I moved away to an island of my own, and now back in the world of *Homo sapiens* I find that my background-noise muscle has atrophied.

I groggily inventory the sounds about me. The lawn sprinkler is going just under my window. My alarm clock clicks on; it is 7:10 now, and two DJs who are either morons or paid to be moronic are laughing at a joke. A motorcycle roars past just as another jet revs for takeoff. Snow tires whine, and a police siren perfectly demonstrates the Doppler effect.

My eyes are wide, almost in fear. I swing my legs to the floor and begin the day already feeling my shoulders tense. I take four aspirin.

BRIEFLY, LET ME DEFINE what it is to readjust to the world of land, and you tell me who's nuts.

Adjusting is:

1. Being assaulted by and not questioning the logic of a girl in a bikini selling milk on a billboard.

2. Allowing others to interrupt meals, baths, sleep, sex, reading, writing, or any other personal activity by making a small object in your home scream and vibrate for your attention.

3. Having to look two or three ways at intersections so that tons of steel, plastic, and glass don't crash into you.

4. Locking doors.

5. Turning on switches or knobs for light and water. Not since times recorded in the beginning of the Bible has it been so easy.

6. Having no sense of the earth: my blinds are drawn, I don't walk outside of my fenced yard, I don't know what tide it is, and I don't know the phase of the moon. The wind and rain mean nothing; they have no affect on me at all.

7. Feeling as if I'm somehow falling behind, not on schedule. In nature I am caught up, whole, and complete.

8. Worrying about collecting small pieces of green paper, and then panicking about how they add up.

9. Not waving at cars you pass, not saying hello to every person you see.

10. And finally, living with drywall. Why would anyone choose to live in a home where a nail won't stay in a wall? And *white walls*? Is this a joke? I personally carry enough dirt on me by the end of a good day to smear shades of gray along thirty feet of wall.

I LOOK THROUGH the wanted pages, but nothing interests me except the truck-driving ads. As the tide no longer pulls on my blood, all that seems to matter is how to keep those numbers before the decimal point. To care about this is pathetic to me, yet what else matters just now? Stephan visits friends and plays on their computers and watches their TVs—we won't have one. Last week he was at his friend's house and was accidentally left behind by two parents and four kids. They went to a baseball game and neither they nor Stephan realized he was forgotten, immobile before the television.

A few things are unchanged. If I look pathetically enough at Wendy she will get her tweezers and groom me. My feelings for her continue to slide up and down a scale whose range includes bubbly teenage excitement, gloom, lust, fear, and joy.

Bear is still always by my side. We like to go into the yard and pee together. Abby continues to exult in a continuous brainless yet blissful moment, and I sometimes envy her.

My relationship with Stephan has grown to include friendship. I am still the authority person, and that seems to be okay with him. He introduces me to his friends as "the evil stepdad," and I introduce him to mine as "the thing that lives with us." We laugh a lot. He continues to be the one who seems to grow when we struggle. I have apologized a few more times. He has always accepted it with grace. I still think that I am lacking some instinct that nature would have provided me if Stephan were my own blood. I encourage him to see his other dad in the hopes that he will find something there that I cannot provide. But is the nourishment one seeks available that way, like at a salad bar? I can only hope. I love him, and that still scares me.

IF THIS WERE FICTION, somewhere near the end there would be a tearful scene that concluded with Stephan and me embracing, possibly after I saved his life. He would realize that I was the best father there was. Wendy would show me that I needed to rejoin civilization after all, and I would have returned, as Thoreau did, a wiser man.

But my life doesn't work like that. There is no swelling music to indicate that I am about to live happily ever after. My story does not come together as Dickens would have it at the end of *Great Expectations*. I live my life on the mainland, in a suburb, surrounded by day-to-day nonfiction. My return to civilization will always strike me as lacking, but for my family. Still, I do not live suspended between the disparity of reality and fiction. I find satisfaction in knowing that I am the author of my own life, and I would rather misspell a word than not have written it.

I do daydream, though, and if I open the windows just right I can get the desert wind to browse through the house like its ocean cousin used to. Way in the distance I can feel the restless murmur of tides licking rocky shores. Like listening to a shell, I think I can hear the waves, but it is really just my own heart.

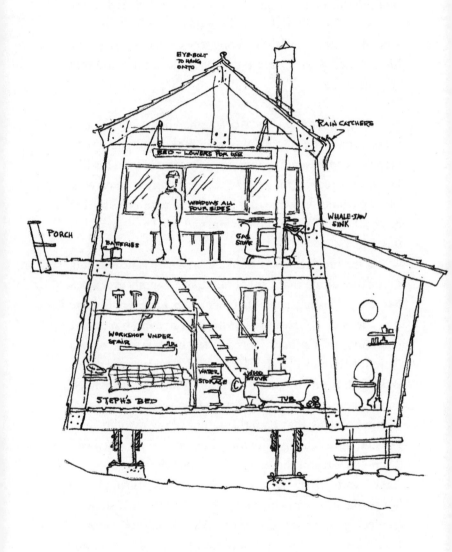

A cross section of our house, as seen by my father.

ACKNOWLEDGMENTS

My thanks to Robbie at the Creative Edge for teaching me how to train all those rebellious electrons, and thank you, Faige, for selling me my first computer, which was, incidentally, full of rebellious electrons. Barge and Karen for ruthless support, Courtney for encouraging my dirty mind, Ilene for keeping me afraid of my dirty mind, Laine for her heart, and Angel for her smile.

Thanks and hugs to my mom, who I miss very much, and love to my dad for standing by me no matter what I step in. *(Please send money.)* To Roger Parrott, Jeff Campbell, and Will Lesh, thank you for sharing your passions, feeding the fire.

Thanks to my editor, Kathy Pories, who cut most of the really offensive parts but left in a few; and to my agent, Brian Defiore, thanks for encouraging those offensive parts.

Thank you, Stephan, for your willingness to train and put up with an untested dad.